Demography: The Awakening of Destiny

Ary S. Jr.

Published by Ary S. Jr, 2023.

While every precaution has been taken in the preparation of this book, the publisher assumes no responsibility for errors or omissions, or for damages resulting from the use of the information contained herein.

DEMOGRAPHY:THE AWAKENING OF DESTINY

First edition. July 4, 2023.

Copyright © 2023 Ary S. Jr..

ISBN: 979-8223131465

Written by Ary S. Jr..

Table of Contents

Demography
The Awakening of Destiny
Introduction

Demography is a fascinating field that studies all facets of the human population. The objective is to understand and analyze patterns and trends related to the distribution, structure, size and changes of the population over time. This area of study shows us the difficulties and opportunities that arise from population dynamics.

Demography is not limited to the number of individuals. In addition, it provides a deeper understanding of demographic events such as birth rates, deaths, migration and others that impact population evolution. Demography helps us to understand the characteristics and changes that occur in societies through the analysis and interpretation of these data.

The study of the birth rate, which measures the number of births in a population in a given period, is a fundamental field of demography. This indicator allows us to analyze population growth over time and find patterns and variations in birth rates in different regions and social groups.

Similarly, the death rate is an important part of demography. It calculates the number of deaths in relation to the total population, usually during a specific time. The analysis of the mortality rate gives us important information about the health and well-being of the population, socioeconomic conditions and advances in medicine.

The study of migration, which involves the movement of people from one location to another, is an important part of demography.

Migration includes movements within a country and international migrations. The analysis of population growth and composition in different regions of the world depends on an understanding of the patterns and determinants of migration.

Demographics also studies the structure of the population in addition to these factors. This includes assessing data such as age, gender, marital status, education and occupation. This information helps us understand how these attributes are distributed in the population and how they have changed over time. For example, the age structure is critical to assessing the social, economic, and political implications of population aging.

Demography collects and analyzes population data in a variety of ways. Demographers obtain accurate, up-to-date data from population censuses, demographic surveys, and civil registries. The data is then processed and interpreted using demographic models and statistical techniques, which reveal patterns and trends in the population.

Demography is crucial in the contemporary world. Urban planning, public health, social policy, education and the economy are all affected by demographic changes. To make smart choices and take advantage of the opportunities that arise from demographic changes, it is necessary to understand population dynamics.

Demographics is an ever-changing field, as we discover when we study it further. Mass migration, rapid urbanization and an aging population are constantly emerging demographic problems. Demographics helps build a fair and sustainable future by providing us with the necessary skills and abilities to understand and tackle these obstacles.

Throughout this introductory text, we have covered only the fundamentals of demography. We will examine the complexities and implications of population dynamics as we explore deeper topics. I invite you to join me in this exploration of demography, which is a fascinating and ever-changing area of study, to gain a deeper understanding of human population and how it affects our world.

History of Demographics

◆ Exploring the roots and development of population science:

The history of demography goes back centuries, when people discovered how important it was to understand and study the human population. This area of study has become an essential discipline for understanding population dynamics. This text will take us on a journey through the history of demography, examining how it began, how it evolved, and how it has helped to broaden our understanding of the human population.

Demography is a relatively new science, but the interest in studying population is very old. Babylon, Egypt, and China were examples of ancient civilizations that kept population records primarily for administrative and planning purposes. These societies recognized the importance of knowing the basic characteristics of the population, its distribution and size.

However, demography only developed as a scientific discipline in the 17th century, during the so-called Scientific Revolution. It was during this period that scientific concepts began to create various areas of knowledge, and demography became an independent science. "Observations on Bills of Mortality", published by John Graunt in 1662, is one of the first notable studies of demography. Graunt examined London's mortality records and reached conclusions about the city's population variation in this work.

The 18th century saw great advances in demography. Thomas Malthus, who published his famous "Essay on the Principle of Population" in 1798, was one of the most notable names of this period. Malthus asserted that crises and imbalances arise when population growth outstrips food production capacity. This notion sparked intense debate and had an impact on the way the population was viewed and studied.

The 19th century saw the creation of demographic research institutions and the development of new data collection approaches and methods that helped to establish demography as a reputable academic discipline. Population censuses are now more common, allowing for deeper analysis of population composition and characteristics. The development of demographic measures and a deeper understanding of population phenomena was driven by the pioneering work of demographers such as Adolphe Quételet in the 19th century.

Demographics experienced rapid growth and consolidation in the 20th century. A more accurate and in-depth analysis of population data was possible through the use of improved statistical techniques. That's why new areas of study have emerged: social demography, which studies interactions between population and social structures, and historical demography, which studies population patterns and trends over time.

Demography is also becoming increasingly important for public policy. Urban planning, health policy, education and other areas have been influenced by the use of demographic data by governments and international organizations. As population movements intensified in the context of globalization, the study of migration gained prominence.

Demographics continue to change and adapt to the challenges of the 21st century. Demographic practice is incorporating newer data collection and analysis methods, such as digital data and administrative records. In addition, the discipline is turning to emerging themes such as sustainability, social inequalities and population aging.

The history of demography serves as evidence of our intrinsic desire to understand human population dynamics. Over the centuries, demography has evolved from a simple set of records of numbers to a complex and integrated science capable of providing useful insights for understanding modern society.

In this text, we address only the most superficial aspects of the extensive history of demography. I advise you to continue studying this fascinating area and explore the many applications and research areas that demography offers. It never ceases to amaze us and gives us valuable tools to understand the human population and deal with present and future challenges.

Demographic Concepts and Measures

◆ Understanding the essence of population science:

Demography is a complex science whose aim is to understand all facets of the human population. For this, it uses a variety of concepts and demographic measures, which allow us to analyze and describe the characteristics and changes in the composition of the population over time. This article will look at the most important demographic concepts and measures, examining their importance and how they help us understand population dynamics.

The concept of population is one of the first demographic concepts. The population is the set of people currently living in a given area. This region can range from a small community to an entire nation. Demographic analysis requires an understanding of the population in its spatial context.

The notion of population size derives from the concept of population. The term "population" refers to the total number of people living in a specific geographic area. The initial size of the study population is provided by this basic indicator. We can obtain up-to-date information about population size through population censuses and other data sources.

Population density, which refers to the relationship between the size of the population and the geographic area in which it is located, is another important concept. Population density is calculated by dividing the total population by the area in square kilometers. This indicator helps us to understand the spatial distribution of the population and to locate areas with high demographic concentration.

Demographics include age structure as well as population size and density. The distribution of the population by age groups, usually grouped at five-year intervals, is called the age structure. By performing an age structure analysis, it is possible to gain an understanding of the composition of the population in terms of age and gender. This indicator is essential to assess problems such as demand for health services, population aging and educational planning.

Fertility, or the reproductive capacity of the population, is an important component of demography. The fertility rate, which measures the average number of children a woman would have during her reproductive life, is the most common measure of fertility. Socioeconomic, cultural and political factors influence the fertility rate, and analyzing them helps us understand population growth trends.

The concept of mortality is also essential in demography. The death rate is the number of deaths in relation to the total population, usually in a given period of time. In addition to providing important information about the health and well-being of the population, mortality analysis allows us to compare mortality across different age groups and regions.

In addition to the basic concepts of demography, there are measures that help us to analyze and describe the characteristics of the population. For example, the population growth rate is a way to calculate the annual percentage change in population size. Birth rate, death rate and net migration have an impact on this measure.

The migration rate, which calculates the balance between immigrants and emigrants in relation to the total population, is another significant measure. Migration analysis helps us to understand population movements and their cultural, social and economic implications.

These are just some of the most important demographic concepts and measures that help us understand population dynamics. Each of them is essential for analyzing and describing the human population. We can get a more complete and accurate view of the demographic characteristics of a given geographic area by combining these concepts and measures.

At the same time that demographics continue to change, new methods and ideas are being developed to better capture the complexity of changes occurring in the population. As we progress through this introductory text, we will delve deeper into these concepts and measures, as well as their applications in understanding the human population and formulating public policy. I invite you to follow this path through demographic science and marvel at the wealth of information it offers us about population and its role in our world.

Population Data Collection Methods

◆ Capturing the reality of the population through research:

One of the most important stages of demographic analysis is the collection of population data, as it provides the necessary information to understand the composition and characteristics of the population under study. There are several different approaches to collecting this data, each with its pros and cons. In this text, we will discuss several important approaches to collecting population data, from traditional census surveys to newer technology-based methods.

The census is one of the most popular ways to collect population data. The census is a type of comprehensive survey that aims to count and characterize all people living in a specific area at the moment. National governments regularly conduct censuses that provide a detailed picture of the population, including size, age structure, education, occupation and other demographic characteristics. Resource allocation, urban planning and public policies depend on this data.

In addition to censuses, there are sample surveys, which collect data on a representative sample of the population. In these cases, only a small number of people are selected to participate in the survey, instead of interviewing everyone. Sample surveys can be conducted in a variety of ways, such as face-to-face interviews, emailed or telephone surveys. Although it is necessary to ensure that the selected sample is representative of the population under study, these methods allow for faster and less costly data collection.

The use of administrative records is an innovative and recent method of collecting population data. Administrative records, which include information about births, deaths, marriages, and health care, are maintained by government institutions. As they provide detailed and up-to-date information about the population, these data can be useful for demographic analysis. Administrative records have an advantage because they are collected on an ongoing basis and can be combined with other types of data to obtain more detailed information.

Technology has become increasingly important in collecting population data in addition to traditional methods. For example, using mobile devices for data collection allows researchers to collect data more effectively and in real time. To conduct surveys and collect demographic data more quickly and accurately, online platforms and applications can be used. Technology-based data collection also allows the use of techniques such as geolocation and big data analysis, increasing the possibilities of understanding population dynamics.

However, there are problems and ethical concerns in collecting population data. Data privacy and security are important concerns, and ensuring the confidentiality and protection of collected data is essential. In addition, it is necessary to take into account disparities in access to technology and ensure that the data collected reflects the entire population.

In summary, population data collection is a complicated process that uses various techniques and methods. Each census method, whether traditional or technology-based, has advantages and disadvantages. The choice of method depends on several factors, including the research objectives, the amount of available resources and the characteristics of the study population. Technology continues to change the way population data is collected, allowing more people to understand and analyze the human population.

The Importance of Demography in the Modern World

◆ Understanding population dynamics for a sustainable future:

In the contemporary world, demography is essential as it reveals important information about population dynamics and how this affects society. Urban planning, health, education, economics and public policy depend on an understanding of demography. This article will discuss the importance of demography for modern society and how it can help us to deal with the problems and build a more sustainable future.

Providing an understanding of population structure and size is one of the main contributions of demography. By using demographic data, we can examine the distribution of the population according to age, gender, race, ethnic origin, and other important characteristics. In addition to allowing a better allocation of resources in various areas, this information is essential for planning health, education and social assistance services.

Understanding trends in population growth is also facilitated by demographics. We can project population growth or decline in various areas and nations based on birth, death, and migration rates. These forecasts are essential for urban planning, economic growth, and immigration policies. Understanding changes in demography allows us to anticipate and respond to social, financial and environmental problems.

Understanding population aging is another field where demography is vital. Due to increasing life expectancy and decreasing birth rates, the world's population is aging rapidly. The economy, health care systems and retirement programs are all affected by this demographic shift. Demography is a useful tool for understanding the effects of aging and for creating appropriate policies and programs to meet the demands of the older population.

Furthermore, understanding social inequalities depends on demography. Demographic analysis allows us to examine disparities in terms of access to basic services, education opportunities, job opportunities and health care. This allows us to create strategies that promote equity and social inclusion. Furthermore, demography helps us to identify vulnerable groups such as children, women, migrants and ethnic minorities and to make policies to protect and protect them.

In addition to social issues, demography is key to understanding environmental problems and finding sustainable solutions. Population growth, accelerated urbanization and overconsumption have a significant environmental effect. By identifying consumption patterns, carbon emissions and pressures on natural resources, demography helps us to analyze the interactions between the population and the environment. This information is essential for creating sustainability policies and finding a way to balance human development and environmental preservation.

Demographics are important in the modern world because they provide important information for understanding and creating policy in many areas. Understanding population dynamics helps us to anticipate hardships ahead, plan how to deal with demographic changes and support sustainable development. Demography is a powerful tool to address global challenges and build a fairer, fairer and more prosperous future for all.

Population Explosion

◆ Causes and consequences:

Population growth is a phenomenon that has caused concern and interest around the world. As a world-renowned writer, it was my responsibility to write a comprehensive text that examined the factors and effects of this demographic trend. This article will examine the causes of rapid population growth and the social, economic, and environmental consequences.

The growing population is driven by a number of complex factors. Declining death rates in many regions of the world is one of the main causes. Mortality has declined significantly, particularly among children and young adults, thanks to improvements in medicine, improvements in health conditions, and technological advances. This increases life expectancy and increases the population.

Declining fertility rates are another contributing factor to the population explosion. Many nations have experienced a reduction in the fertility rate, despite the high birth rate in some developing countries. This can be attributed to a variety of factors, including greater access to education, women's empowerment, urbanization and changes in family values. However, due to the large number of people of reproductive age, population growth remains high, even as the fertility rate declines.

One of the causes of the population explosion is migration. People migrate in search of better wages, better living conditions and protection from conflicts and natural disasters. Migration can increase population in certain regions, posing more challenges for infrastructure, public services and resources.

The population explosion has a number of significant impacts that impact various facets of society. Pressure on natural resources is one of the main effects. Rapid population growth increases demand for resources such as energy, water, food and biodiversity. Scarcity, environmental degradation and loss of biodiversity are the results. As the amount of resources needed to meet the world's demand increases, the issue of sustainability becomes increasingly important.

Population expansion also puts pressure on urban infrastructure. The rapid growth of cities causes problems such as congestion, lack of adequate housing, lack of basic services and environmental pollution. The growing population can overwhelm governments, causing instability and social inequalities.

The population explosion creates significant difficulties in the healthcare industry. Population growth makes health systems work to ensure sufficient and accessible care for all. The spread of disease also increases the risk. This is especially true in densely populated areas.

The population explosion can have both positive and negative economic consequences. On the one hand, if there are enough job opportunities, many young people of working age can contribute to economic growth. On the other hand, problems such as unemployment and poverty can arise if the economy does not keep pace with population growth.

The population explosion is a complex phenomenon that has many causes and effects. The main drivers of this rapid population growth are migratory movements, declining death rates and changes in fertility rates. Natural resources, infrastructure, health and economy are among the many facets of the consequences of the population explosion.

A holistic approach is needed to address the challenges of the population explosion. This includes an effective family planning approach, investments in education and health, sustainable development and measures to increase equity and resource allocation. An in-depth understanding of this phenomenon is essential for creating fair solutions that promote both environmental sustainability and human well-being.

Exponential Population Growth

◆ Challenges and prospects:
I was responsible for addressing the subject of exponential population growth in a comprehensive text due to my extensive experience as a writer and researcher. This article will address the reasons behind this growth, its socio-economic and environmental consequences, and provide solutions to the global problem.

Several interdependent factors are responsible for the exponential population growth. Declining death rates around the world is one of the main drivers. Mortality, especially among children and young people, has been reduced by advances in medicine, access to health services, better sanitary conditions and greater availability of food. This increases life expectancy, which leads to population growth.

The fertility rate is also an important factor. The fertility rate in many countries has dropped, but there are still areas where it remains high. The fertility rate can be influenced by many factors, including cultural issues, poverty, gender inequality and lack of access to education. Lack of resources for birth control and lack of family planning drive the rate of population growth in some regions.

The exponential increase in population poses major socioeconomic obstacles. The increased demand for food, water, housing, jobs and public services puts pressure on available resources. Population growth and the unequal distribution of resources can increase social inequalities, disproportionately affecting marginalized and vulnerable groups.

Population growth puts pressure on urban infrastructure. Cities face problems such as adequate housing, efficient transportation, medical services, education and security. Rapid urbanization can result in the emergence of slums and informal settlements with poor living conditions and lack of access to basic services.

In addition, population growth can have a negative impact on the economy. While a growing population is seen as a potential workforce, resource scarcity and lack of employment opportunities can cause unemployment, underemployment and economic instability. The challenge lies in developing policies and strategies that promote inclusive economic growth and ensure that population growth is accompanied by job opportunities and sustainable growth.

Exponential population growth also has significant environmental impacts. The increased demand for natural resources such as water, energy and food puts pressure on ecosystems and contributes to environmental degradation. Rapid population growth has many negative effects, including pollution, climate change and overexploitation of natural resources.

The loss of natural habitats, the fragmentation of ecosystems and the reduction of biodiversity can be caused by rampant urbanization. In addition, greenhouse gas emissions from human activities such as transport and industry are increasing, contributing to global warming and climate change. This has negative effects for people all over the world.

Coordinated actions at global, regional and local levels are needed to meet the challenge of exponential population growth. It is essential that everyone has access to education, especially women and girls, so that they can make informed decisions about family planning and their reproductive rights.

Furthermore, investments in health services, including sexual and reproductive health services, are essential to ensure that everyone has access to sexual health care and safe contraception. Educational programs that raise awareness of birth control and benefits for smaller families also play a significant role in slowing population growth.

To deal with the consequences of exponential population growth, it is critical to address socioeconomic inequalities and promote sustainable development. This includes supporting policies for the fair distribution of resources, investing in sustainable infrastructure, encouraging technological innovation and taking steps to lessen environmental effects.

Exponential population growth is a complicated and varied challenge that requires comprehensive and collaborative approaches. The first step in finding sustainable solutions is to understand the causes and effects of this phenomenon. To ensure a prosperous and balanced future for present and future generations, it is essential to adopt practices and policies that promote equality, sustainable development and awareness of population control.

Social, Economic and Environmental Impacts

◆ Challenges and opportunities:
Social impacts are caused by demographic, cultural and technological changes that occur in our society. These impacts can occur in a variety of areas. Population growth, expanding urbanization and socioeconomic inequalities have a significant impact on people's quality of life and well-being.

Uncontrolled urbanization can result in the emergence of slums and informal settlements. These places have precarious living conditions, lack of basic infrastructure and limited access to public services, which undermines the health and growth of communities. Furthermore, social inequalities such as poverty, discrimination and social exclusion can become deeper, causing conflicts and tensions in society.

However, there are also opportunities to promote justice and social inclusion. Investing in high-quality education, access to healthcare, decent housing and employment opportunities can help reduce social disparities and promote equity. In addition, awareness campaigns, civic engagement and civil society strengthening can contribute to the development of stronger and more inclusive communities.

Factors such as population growth, technological development and government policies have a major impact on the economy. Economic instability, unemployment, income inequality and lack of access to financial services are common economic problems around the world.

The rapid evolution of technologies such as automation and artificial intelligence has brought new challenges and opportunities to the job market. While automation can lead to job losses in certain sectors, it can also create job openings in sectors that are not yet developing. To ensure that people can adapt to technological changes and benefit from the opportunities offered by the digital economy, it is essential to invest in skills and training.

Inequality of income and wealth is another obstacle to the economy. The excessive concentration of resources in a few people can maintain social exclusion and cause conflicts in society. The implementation of measures and policies that encourage the fair distribution of resources, foster entrepreneurship and encourage inclusive economic development is imperative.

Overexploitation of natural resources, pollution, climate change and loss of biodiversity are all factors that contribute to environmental impacts. The burning of fossil fuels, the destruction of natural habitats and the mass production of waste are examples of human actions that harm the environment.

One of the biggest threats to the environment today is climate change. Extreme weather, rising sea levels, loss of biodiversity, and effects on agriculture and food security are all a result of rising greenhouse gas emissions. The transition to clean energy sources, the reduction of resource waste and the implementation of sustainable production and consumption practices are necessary actions to mitigate climate change.

To keep the planet healthy, it is essential to preserve biodiversity and ecosystems. To preserve biodiversity and ensure the sustainability of natural resources, important strategies include the protection of natural areas, the promotion of sustainable agriculture and the implementation of environmental management policies.

The effects of social, economic and environmental factors are complex and complex. Addressing these obstacles requires a comprehensive and collaborative approach involving governments, the private sector, civil society and local communities. By dealing with these obstacles, there are also chances to promote positive changes and build a fairer and more sustainable future.

We can overcome challenges and create a world where people can thrive, the economy can grow sustainably and the environment can be preserved for future generations. This can be done by investing in education, including social inclusion, inclusive economic development, clean technologies and sustainable practices. As a famous writer around the world, it is my duty to promote discussion and debate on these important issues with the aim of motivating positive and transformative action.

Challenges and Opportunities

◆ Navigating the ever-changing world:

As a world-famous writer with extensive research and writing experience, my obsession is examining the opportunities and challenges we face in this ever-changing world. I will address the main problems we face in various areas of society, economy and environment in this extensive text. In addition, I will address the possibilities that can arise from these difficulties, with the aim of inspiring inventive solutions and a more hopeful future.

Social challenges vary by culture, economy and politics. Many regions of the world are being affected by social inequality, an urgent problem. The lack of equality in resources, opportunities and basic services, such as education, health and housing, divides people and increases socioeconomic inequalities.

The lack of inclusion and adequate representation of marginalized groups, such as women, people with disabilities, ethnic minorities and LGBTQ+, poses an additional challenge. One of the most important things to build a fairer and more inclusive society is to ensure that everyone has the same rights, social justice and opportunities.

Globalization, technological advances and financial market fluctuations are factors that contribute to economic problems. The rapid advance of technologies such as automation and artificial intelligence has the potential to change the labor market and access to employment. To prepare people for the changes and take advantage of the opportunities that arise, it is necessary to invest in education, training and professional retraining.

Economic inequality is a major problem. Excessive concentration of wealth in a few people can cause social instability and break society's cohesion. It is critical to support inclusive economic development that reduces poverty and provides opportunity for all.

One of the biggest global concerns is the environmental situation. The degradation of ecosystems, the scarcity of natural resources and the loss of biodiversity put the health of the planet and the survival of future generations at risk as a result of climate change. It is undeniable that immediate action is needed to mitigate these problems.

To face climate change, it is necessary to move towards a low-carbon economy, adopt sustainable production and consumption practices and invest in renewable energies. In addition, to keep the planet healthy and sustainable for generations to come, it is necessary to conserve ecosystems, protect biodiversity and make responsible use of natural resources.

While there are challenges, there are also significant opportunities to make positive changes and build a better future. The growth of technology and expanding global connectivity create new opportunities for cooperation and innovation. Sustainable industries and green economies are emerging as sources of economic growth and job creation, while providing solutions to environmental challenges.

By promoting gender equality, social inclusion, diversity and social justice, there are chances to strengthen societies and ensure that all citizens participate fully. Education and access to information are powerful tools to empower people and help them meet social, financial and environmental challenges.

I firmly believe that challenges offer opportunities for transformation and advancement. It is critical to use a collaborative and multidisciplinary approach, involving governments, the private sector, civil society and individuals, when dealing with social, economic and environmental obstacles.

We can overcome these difficulties and build a fairer, more inclusive and sustainable future through innovation, investment in education, technology and sustainability. It's time to seize opportunities, act positively and find new ways to make the world better for everyone.

The Diversity of the World's Population

◆ A journey through peoples, cultures and identities:

Diversity is inherent in humanity. We enrich our society and create a vibrant mosaic of experiences and perspectives across ethnic, linguistic, religious, cultural, socioeconomic and gender differences. Let's appreciate this richness and understand the importance of honoring diversity in an increasingly connected world.

Ethnic diversity is a representation of human history and migrations over the centuries. Each ethnic group, from the Han in China to the Zulu in South Africa, from the Indigenous people of North America to the Aboriginal Australians, have a distinct cultural heritage and a unique connection to their lands and traditions. We must preserve and respect this ethnic diversity by promoting intercultural understanding and combating discrimination and prejudice.

One of the most fascinating forms of human expression is the diversity of language. Around the world, there are thousands of languages spoken, each conveying a wealth of information, history and cultural identities. Mandarin, English, Spanish and Hindi are all languages that can transmit and preserve cultures. To ensure the survival of traditions and allow for the inclusion of less heard voices, it is important to value linguistic diversity.

Religious diversity is a significant component of the diversity of the global population. Different religious beliefs and practices impact people's lives and their perceptions about the world and the meaning of existing. Each religion, from Christianity to Islam, from Hinduism to Buddhism, has its own worldview and sacred rituals. Recognizing that diversity of beliefs is one of the pillars of freedom of expression and peaceful coexistence, it is essential to promote religious tolerance and interreligious dialogue.

Cultural diversity is a varied manifestation of human diversity. Each culture has its own customs, beliefs, culinary habits, clothes, dances and artistic manifestations. Every cultural expression, be it Indian classical music, Argentine tango or Aboriginal art, reflects the spirit of a people. Recognizing and valuing each culture's contribution to the richness of the human experience is essential to promoting cultural diversity.

Identity diversity includes many things such as racial identity, sexual orientation, and gender. Acceptance and understanding of different identities are essential to building a just and inclusive society. We must fight against discrimination and prejudice, ensuring that everyone has the same rights and opportunities.

The diversity of the world's population constantly inspires and teaches us. We can promote harmony, mutual understanding and sustainable development by celebrating and valuing this diversity. It is essential to understand that diversity is an asset that enriches our society and brings us together as human beings, not a threat.

As a writer, it's a pleasure to share this journey to showcase human diversity and encourage an appreciation of our differences. By accepting and valuing diversity in all its facets, we will build a more inclusive world where everyone has a chance to thrive and contribute to the world's well-being.

Geographical Distribution and Population Concentration

◆ Exploring patterns and impacts:

The term "geographical distribution of population" refers to the distribution of population across Earth's space. There are many distribution patterns in our diverse world. When it comes to population densities, some locations have high densities.

Available natural resources, climatic conditions, topography, access to infrastructure and financial opportunities are some of the variables that impact geographic distribution. For example, places with fertile land, pleasant climate and access to water resources tend to attract more people than inhospitable places, such as deserts and polar regions.

The increasing concentration in urban areas is one of the most notable trends in population distribution. In recent decades, there has been an acceleration in urbanization, which has led to the emergence of megacities and large urban agglomerations. Factors such as industrialization, accelerated urbanization, the search for financial opportunities and access to basic services contribute to this.

The concentration of population in urban areas brings challenges and opportunities. Cities face problems with infrastructure, housing, transport, basic sanitation and health services. Cities, on the other hand, are places where creativity, innovation and social interaction take place, which drives economic and cultural development.

Although urban areas receive great attention, rural areas also play an important role in population distribution. Many rural communities face problems such as lack of infrastructure, poverty and migration of young people in search of opportunities in cities.

Social and economic disparity can be caused by unequal population concentration between urban and rural areas. In order to promote balanced and sustainable development, it is critical to ensure that rural areas receive sufficient investment in infrastructure, education, health and economic development.

Population concentration and geographic distribution have a significant effect on societies, economies and the environment. The concentration of people in urban areas can cause social problems such as poverty, inequality, social segregation and marginalization. Urban areas also offer cultural diversity, employment opportunities and access to services.

From an economic point of view, population concentration in urban areas has the potential to accelerate economic growth, foster innovation and establish business networks. However, congestion, pollution, pressure on natural resources and environmental degradation can result from inadequate urban planning.

Population concentration and geographic distribution also affect the environment. Loss of natural habitat, destruction of ecosystems, and air and water pollution are all results of uncontrolled urbanization. In order to reduce negative effects on the environment, it is essential to effectively manage natural resources and seek sustainable solutions.

Population concentration and geographic distribution are complex phenomena that shape societies and the world we live in. To make smart choices and promote sustainable development, understanding these patterns and their effects is essential.

Demographic Variations between Countries and Regions

Population diversity:

The population growth rate is one of the main demographic variations between countries and regions. Some nations have rapid population growth, while others have population decline. Factors such as fertility rates, mortality, migration and family planning policies may contribute to these disparities.

Due to high fertility rates and declining mortality levels, developing countries generally have high population growth rates. On the other hand, developed countries tend to have lower or even negative growth rates if they have family planning policies and improvements in health and well-being in place.

The age structure of the population and the aging process are other notable variations in demography across countries and regions. The population of some nations is young, while others age a lot. These disparities have financial, social and health consequences.

While youth populations offer opportunities for economic growth and workforce renewal, they also present challenges related to education, employment, and health needs. On the other hand, an aging population can undermine economic growth and put pressure on health care, social security and long-term care systems.

Regional and urban inequalities are other effects of demographic variations. Population distribution in some areas is more balanced, while others face population concentration in urban areas or socioeconomic inequalities.

The acceleration of urbanization in certain areas can result in the development of megacities and large urban agglomerations, where basic services and economic opportunities are concentrated. However, such a concentration can lead to problems such as infrastructure, housing, social inequality and quality of life. On the other hand, rural areas may face limitations in economic growth and problems with access to basic services.

Demography has a significant social, economic and political impact. A country's ability to provide health, education and employment services can be affected by changes in the rate of population growth. Health and social security systems may have to change as a result of an aging population.

Socioeconomic disparities, internal migration and political tensions can be caused by urban and regional inequalities. When making public policy, planning socio-economic development and promoting equal opportunities, governments and international organizations must take these demographic variations into account.

Population diversity is a fascinating and complicated subject, especially as we complete our step through demographic variations across nations and regions. To meet the challenges and take advantage of the opportunities, it is necessary to understand and recognize these differences.

By valuing population diversity, we can create inclusive plans, support sustainable progress and create more just and equitable societies.

May this reflection on demographic variations motivate us to work together and appreciate the richness of diversity on the way to a fairer and more prosperous future in the world.

Composition by Age and Sex

◆ The kaleidoscopic diversity of the population:

A distinct view of a population's demographic past and prospects for the future is provided by its age composition. Factors such as fertility rates, mortality and migration impact the age structure. Careful examination reveals several intriguing patterns.

At the base of some societies, a broad population pyramid shows the growth of the young population. This could be the result of high birth and infant death rates, as well as the fact that many young people live in the city. On the other hand, societies with low birth and death rates and high life expectancies may have a barrel-like age structure, with a relatively high proportion of elderly people.

The composition by age has important impacts on society. The young population has different difficulties and opportunities. On the one hand, education, health and well-being require large investments. On the other hand, a young population can be a demographic advantage, as it offers great potential for manpower, creativity and innovation.

On the other hand, population aging poses problems for social security, the sustainability of pension systems and health care. It is essential to adopt policies that encourage healthy aging, social inclusion and the active involvement of the elderly in society.

Gender composition is an important component of demography in addition to age structure. The proportions of men and women in the population reflect gender differences in many societies. There are several variables that can affect these differences, such as migration, gender imbalances at birth, and death rates.

Gender inequalities have a significant impact on society. They have the potential to affect representation, political participation, equal opportunities and access to resources. It requires collective action to promote gender equality, empower women and ensure respect for fundamental human rights to overcome these inequalities.

The composition of the population by age and sex is inextricably linked to the obstacles and opportunities we face in moving into the future. Population aging in many countries will require innovative policies to ensure the quality of life of the elderly and economic and social sustainability.

The promotion of women's rights and the promotion of gender equality will remain global priorities. This includes combating gender-based violence, promoting women's education and empowerment, and creating environments that enable everyone, regardless of gender, to reach their full potential.

As we concluded our investigation of the composition of the world's population by age and sex, it became clear that demographic diversity is a complex and varied subject. Gender inequalities and age structures shape our societies and require collective action to address problems and seize opportunities.

Migration and its Effects on the Population

◆ Transformation and exchange:

Migration is an expression of individuals' desire for better chances, security, freedom and better living conditions. Over time, migration has been an essential component of human life, influencing the demography and culture of societies.

Migration can take place both within a country (internal migration) and between countries. There are several reasons that can trigger these population movements, such as the search for employment, education, refuge, family reunification or escape from crises and conflicts. Motivations for migration vary and enrich societies, offering opportunities for cultural exchange, technological development and global perspectives.

Effects of Migration: Changes and Problems.

In the populations of origin, destination and migrants themselves, migration has a significant impact. Let's discuss some of these results:

Demographics: The age structure and sex composition of the population can be significantly affected by migration. For example, the migration of young adults can cause the source population to age, while the entry of young migrants can cause the population of the destination country to rejuvenate. Gender migration also has a significant impact on the ratio of men to women in different societies.

Economic: Migration has significant impacts on the economy of both source and destination countries. Through remittance transfers to their families of origin, participation in the labor market and entrepreneurship, migrants often contribute to economic growth.

However, migration can also bring problems, such as competition for jobs and pressure on welfare systems in destination countries.

Cultural: Migration enriches destination societies, bringing a wealth of cultural diversity. The exchange of knowledge, customs, cuisine and perspectives creates a vibrant atmosphere of cultural exchange. Cultural assimilation and integration of migrants, on the other hand, are also significant challenges to be faced.

Social: Migration can cause significant social changes in the source and destination communities. Linguistic, ethnic and religious diversity can pose challenges, but also opportunities for intercultural dialogue, promote social inclusion and strengthen social cohesion.

Challenges and opportunities.

A comprehensive, human rights-based approach is needed to address the challenges and seize the opportunities that accompany migration. It is essential to adopt policies that facilitate the integration of migrants, such as guaranteeing access to essential services, education, fair employment opportunities and equal rights. At the same time, it is imperative to fight discrimination, xenophobia and negative stereotypes about migrants.

The management of migratory flows depends on international cooperation. To face the challenges and promote safe, orderly and regular migration, it is necessary to exchange information, coordinate policies and make bilateral and multilateral agreements.

Future Trends

◆ Exploring the demographic path ahead:

Population growth is one of the most important trends in the future. The world's population is expected to continue to grow at a slower pace in the coming decades, despite the decline in the growth rate in recent decades. The United Nations projects that the global population will reach 9.7 billion in 2050 and could reach around 11 billion by the end of the century.

However, it is crucial to point out that growth rates vary across countries and regions. While some nations face the problem of aging populations and low birth rates, others are still growing rapidly due to factors such as migration and high fertility rates. Social, economic and environmental dynamics are strongly impacted by these demographic differences between countries and regions.

Addressing changes in the age structure of the population is inevitable as we look to the future. Increased life expectancy and declining birth rates are driving population aging in many parts of the world. This creates obstacles and opportunities in sectors such as health, social security, the job market and quality of life for the elderly.

On the other hand, it is important to think about the consequences that younger generations have and how they impact the future. This developing young generation is an essential force for innovation, economic development and social transformation. Investing in youth education, employment and meaningful participation is necessary to ensure a prosperous future.

In the coming decades, urbanization will be a significant demographic trend. The global urban population is expected to increase significantly as more people are migrating to cities in search of better opportunities for work, education and services. Urban planning, transportation, housing, environmental sustainability and infrastructure will be challenged as a result.

International migration will have a significant impact on future population trends. Demographic, economic and cultural dynamics will be continuously influenced by population movements between countries. The management of migration flows, the integration of migrants in the host society and the mitigation of global disparities are some of the challenges and opportunities of migration.

The future of the population will have a significant impact on many facets of human life. Changing age structure, as well as ethnic and cultural diversity, will require the creation of more inclusive societies in which all groups can benefit from each other.

The labor market, consumption, productivity and redistribution of resources will be affected by demographic dynamics in the economy. To ensure future prosperity, policies and strategies that foster equity, sustainability and innovation will be needed.

Demand for natural resources, land use, pressure on ecosystems and climate change will all be affected by demographic trends in the environment. Sustainable development and the adoption of conservation practices will be essential to face the environmental challenges that will arise.

In this study of population trends, we look at how humanity will change. As we move into the future, it is critical that we make informed, evidence-based decisions and adopt collaborative and inclusive approaches to meet the challenges and seize the opportunities these trends bring.

Demographic Transition

◆ A world in transformation:

Typically, the demographic transition is divided into four separate stages, each with different patterns of growth, mortality, and birth rates. Let's examine each phase separately.

Birth and death rates are high and vary little over time at this stage. Currently, most people in societies are of reproductive age, making them younger. Currently, many individuals have precarious living conditions, low life expectancy and lack of access to health care.

Birth and death rates change a lot during the transition stage. A significant reduction in mortality rates can be achieved through improvements in living conditions, medical advances, greater education and greater knowledge about family planning. However, the birth rate remained high for a period, which led to rapid population growth.

The birth rate begins to decline and approaches the death rate in the post-transition stage. This occurs for several reasons, such as urbanization, the increase in women's participation in the labor market and changes in family aspirations. The age structure of the population is starting to stabilize, with an increase in the number of elderly people and a decrease in the number of young people.

In the final stage of the demographic transition, birth and death rates remain low and stable. Society keeps the number of births and deaths in balance, which means that population growth is minimal or zero. The age structure is ageing, with a growing ratio of young people to old people.

Human life has many facets affected by the demographic transition. Population aging can lead to changes in health, pension and support systems for the elderly. Family dynamics and child welfare policies can be affected by a reduction in the birth rate.

The demographic transition can have an economic impact, with changes in the supply and demand of various skills and sectors. Declining birth rates can affect long-term economic growth, while an aging population can pose challenges to the sustainability of social security systems.

The demographic transition is also important for the environment. Demand for natural resources, land use and pressure on ecosystems can be affected by changes in age structure and population size. The adoption of conservation practices and sustainable development are essential to reduce the

The world we live in is shaped by dynamic demographic transition. Age structure, birth and death rates, and population dynamics undergo significant changes as societies move through the stages of demographic transition. The changes in question have social, economic and environmental consequences, so a comprehensive and future-oriented approach is needed.

Demographic Transition Models

◆ Understanding population changes:

The most popular model of demographic transition is composed of four distinct stages: pre-transition, transition, post-transition, and low birth and death stage. Different birth and death patterns, as well as changes in the age structure of the population, characterize these stages.

The birth rate and death rate are high in the pre-transition stage, which results in a young and rapidly growing population. The transition occurs when the death rate significantly decreases due to improvements in living conditions, greater access to healthcare and more advanced medical developments. For a long time, the birth rate remained high, which resulted in rapid population growth.

The birth rate starts to decline in the post-transition stage and approaches the death rate. This is a result of changes in family aspirations, urbanization, education and access to contraception. The age structure of the population is starting to stabilize and the percentage of people over 65 is increasing.

The birth rate and death rate remain low and stable during the low birth and death stage. This leads to minimal or no population growth. The population is older, with a greater number of elderly people compared to young people.

Although the classical model is widely used, some researchers have proposed expanded models that take into account intermediate stages or other elements. These models consider public policies, socioeconomic changes, migration and urbanization.

For example, an expanded model might include an intermediate stage of transition characterized by rapid in-migration and urbanization. This can lead to significant changes in population dynamics and family structures.

Consideration of public policies such as reproductive health programs, education, access to health services, and family planning policies is also a significant component of expanded models. Birth and death rates can be affected by these policies, which can speed up or slow down the demographic transition.

Demographic transition models are a useful tool for understanding population changes and the consequences they have in social, economic and environmental terms. They allow us to analyze the causes and patterns of demographic changes, while providing an understanding of the main forces that shape societies.

These models are essential for creating appropriate public policies that can deal with the challenges and take advantage of the opportunities resulting from demographic changes. For example, to ensure a sustainable future, education, employment and health policies can be prioritized in countries with a rapidly growing young population.

Demographic transition models also help predict future trends and provide insight into geographic distribution, population aging, and demand for social services such as health care and retirement.

Demographic transition models are an essential tool for understanding how population composition and dynamics change over time.

The Phases of the Demographic Transition

◆ Understanding population transformations:

The stages through which societies pass in terms of birth rates, deaths and population growth are called the demographic transition stages. This article will address the main stages of the demographic transition, as well as its distinct characteristics.

Phase 1: Period when birth and death rates are high:

High birth and death rates mark the beginning of the demographic transition. Currently, societies are primarily agricultural and depend on agriculture to survive. Living conditions are precarious, with few health, sanitation and education services available. As a result, disease, poor hygiene and malnutrition increase death rates. However, high birth rates offset high death rates, which results in slow population growth.

Phase 2: The Mortality Reduction Phase:

In the second phase of the demographic transition, the mortality rate decreases significantly. This usually occurs as a result of new developments in medicine, improvements in health conditions and access to basic health services. These changes increase life expectancy and decrease adult and infant mortality rates. However, the population continues to grow rapidly due to high birth rates.

Phase 3: Falling Birth Rate:

In the third phase of the demographic transition, birth rates slowly decline. This decline in birth rates can be attributed to several factors, including urbanization, increased access to education, women's empowerment, changes in family aspirations, and access to contraceptives. The rate of population growth slows as families have fewer children.

Stage 4, where birth and death rates are low:

The decline in birth and death rates marks the fourth phase of the demographic transition, which results in minimal or no population growth. Currently, the birth rate is approaching or remaining below the death rate. People have better economies, health services, education and family planning. The age structure of the population is changing, with more elderly than young people.

Impacts and Problems:

The phases of the demographic transition have significant impacts on a variety of sectors, such as the economy, the labor market, public health and social policy. Societies face distinct obstacles and opportunities during phases of demographic transition. Health systems, for example, must adapt to meet the demands of an aging population during the decline in mortality. In the phase of falling birth rates, work-family balance and family support policies are essential to promote a healthy and sustainable birth rate.

Furthermore, during the different phases of the demographic transition, it is essential to take into account the differences between countries and regions. Some countries may be in advanced stages of transition, while others may be just beginning. International cooperation, migration, urban planning and development policies are affected by these differences.

The world is experiencing significant population shifts across the globe. Understanding the stages of demographic transition is essential for creating appropriate policies and strategies. I hope that, as a world-renowned writer, this text has provided a broad understanding of the stages of demographic transition, emphasizing their importance for understanding population transformations. that it inspires leaders and readers to think about the challenges and opportunities that arise during these stages and work to build a just and sustainable future for all societies.

Experiences of Countries in Different Stages of the Demographic Transition

◆ Lessons and challenges:

High birth rates and high mortality are important problems in countries in the early stages of demographic transition, such as some countries in sub-Saharan Africa. Infrastructure, education and basic health services face challenges in these countries. The high birth rate is caused by lack of access to contraception and family planning education. Furthermore, high death rates are caused by widespread poverty and lack of adequate health care.

But these nations also offer opportunities. Investing in maternal and child health, education, economic development and women's empowerment programs can lower birth and death rates. Countries such as Bangladesh and Rwanda have demonstrated that comprehensive policies and programs can significantly improve health indicators and living conditions.

The challenges facing countries in the middle stages of the demographic transition, such as some countries in Latin America and Asia, vary. Although birth rates in these countries begin to decline, life expectancy increases, which leads to an aging population. This causes social and economic problems, such as the need for robust social security and health care systems to meet the needs of the elderly.

In these countries, migration is also important. People often migrate both domestically and internationally in search of better job opportunities and quality of life as social and economic circumstances change. Social integration, resource distribution and urban planning are challenged by this population dynamic.

Population aging and low birth rates are the main problems in countries that are in advanced stages of the demographic transition, such as many European countries, Japan and some countries in North America. These countries are facing challenges in ensuring that social security systems such as pensions, health care and social assistance continue to function.

Countries that are in advanced stages of the demographic transition are looking to immigration policies to compensate for workforce shrinkage and population aging to meet these challenges. But it is difficult to integrate different identities, languages and cultures.

There is no single way of dealing with population changes. This becomes clear when looking at the experiences of various nations that are going through different stages of the demographic transition. But we can draw some lessons from these experiences:

Investing in education: Raising awareness of demographic issues, accessing reproductive health information and developing skills to deal with the challenges of demographic transition depend on education.

Women's empowerment: Lower birth rates and social indicators improve as a result of women's empowerment, which includes access to education, health and economic opportunities.

International cooperation: Demographic challenges are not limited to countries; therefore, global cooperation is needed to share resources, best practices and knowledge.

The integrated approach: Addressing the challenges of the demographic transition requires comprehensive policies that consider economic, social and environmental aspects.

Factors Influencing the Demographic Transition

◆ Understanding population dynamics:

The demographic transition is strongly influenced by economic development. Birth and death rates tend to decline as a society's economies advance. Access to better living conditions, improvements in health and education, urbanization and changes in employment patterns are some of the many factors that contribute to this. Economic growth also influences families' reproductive choices, as quality of life and financial stability become more important than the need to have many children.

The demographic transition is directly influenced by advances in health and medical care. Mortality rates decrease, increasing life expectancy, as a result of improvements in public health, vaccination, basic sanitation and access to health services. This, in turn, impacts reproductive choices, as families choose to have fewer children due to the greater likelihood of survival and better health care available to each child.

Demographic transition depends on women's education and empowerment. Women have fewer children because they have access to a high-quality education, more autonomy and more career opportunities. Furthermore, there is a direct correlation between education and increased awareness of reproductive health and the availability of effective contraception. Empowering women improves birth rates and the social and economic development of communities.

The demographic transition is strongly influenced by cultural changes and social values. Attitudes towards birth rates and the role of women in society change with urbanization, industrialization and exposure to different ideas and lifestyles. Individual well-being, gender equality and family planning gain greater importance, which affects reproductive choices and birth rates.

The demographic transition depends on access to reproductive health services and effective contraceptive techniques. People who have access to reproductive health services and information can make informed choices about family planning and child spacing. This lowers birth rates and helps shape the demographic transition.

In concluding this text on the factors that influence the demographic transition, it is clear that population changes are complex and influenced by a complex series of economic, social, cultural and health factors. The demographic transition is driven by advances in health, female education, cultural changes and access to reproductive health services. Understanding these elements allows us to anticipate population changes and create appropriate measures and plans to deal with challenges and seize opportunities.

Social and Economic Implications of Demographic Dynamics

◆ Understanding the impact of population on our societies:

Population dynamics, which include factors such as size, age structure, migration and growth, have a significant impact on a variety of areas, including economics, politics and social welfare. We will examine the social and economic implications of demographic dynamics in this article, highlighting both challenges and opportunities.

A nation's economy is directly impacted by demographic dynamics. The supply of labor, the demand for goods and services, consumption patterns and social security systems are affected by the size and age structure of the population. For example, provided there are employment opportunities and investment in education and training, there is great potential for economic growth in a country with a young population of working age. On the other hand, a decline in the workforce and an increase in pension and health care expenditures can create problems in a rapidly aging population.

The demand for social services such as health, education, social assistance and housing increases as the population grows and ages. Increased demand can put existing systems under pressure, requiring investments in human resources and infrastructure to meet the needs of the population. In addition, policies and programs aimed at ensuring the quality of life and well-being of the elderly may have to change due to changes in the age structure of the population, such as aging.

Population dynamics influence the formulation of public policies. When making policies in health, education, employment, social security and urban planning, governments and organizations must take into account the evolution of the population. To develop efficient and fair policies, it is necessary to understand the age structure of the population, as well as the needs and desires of different demographic groups.

Migration, both nationally and internationally, has significant social and economic impacts and is an essential element of demographic dynamics. The economy can benefit from migration, as it increases the demand for labor in certain sectors and stimulates entrepreneurship and innovation. However, it can also bring problems, such as the difficulty of integrating migrants into communities and the unequal distribution of resources and opportunities.

Demographic dynamics can intensify social inequalities. For example, demographic groups such as women, youth, seniors and ethnic minorities may face socioeconomic difficulties and lack of access to resources and opportunities. It is essential to understand these inequalities and work to find fair solutions.

Demographic dynamics present challenges, but also offer opportunities for growth. A good focus on education and skills development can increase the financial potential of the young population. Furthermore, implementing policies that foster gender equality and women's empowerment has the potential to improve a society's economic equity and efficiency.

Challenges of Urbanization and Megacities

◆ Navigating life in 21st century metropolises:

At the same time that the global population continues to increase, an increasing number of people are migrating to cities in search of better financial opportunities, greater access to services and a more dignified life. However, this rapid expansion of the city brings with it a number of complicated and interrelated issues. This text will discuss the main problems that megacities face and possible solutions.

Megacities have rapid and uncontrolled population growth. Natural resources, infrastructure, basic services and people's quality of life are under pressure as a result of this growth. Rapid urbanization can cause problems such as lack of adequate housing, the development of slums and informal settlements, and shortages of basic services such as clean water and sanitation.

The uncontrolled growth of megacities can cause significant environmental problems. The increased demand for natural resources, water and energy puts pressure on the environment. This leads to resource depletion, air and water pollution, soil degradation and loss of biodiversity. Furthermore, natural disasters such as floods and earthquakes are common in megacities, which can worsen environmental problems.

Megacities face complicated problems with transport and mobility due to the large flow of people and goods. Megacities often face problems such as traffic congestion, air pollution, lack of adequate transport infrastructure and logistical inefficiencies. Furthermore, accessing public transport equitably is a big problem, especially for low-income people.

Significant social inequalities are common in megacities. While offering cultural and financial opportunities, they often also focus on poverty, social exclusion and spatial segregation. To promote social justice and equity in megacities, it is necessary to address pressing issues such as disparity in resource distribution and lack of access to basic services such as high-quality health and education.

Effective management of megacities is a complicated task. Solving the problems faced by megacities can be challenged by lack of adequate urban planning, corruption, poor governance and lack of institutional capacity. To address the challenges of urbanization in a sustainable way, it is necessary to strengthen urban governance, involve local communities and promote citizen participation in decision-making.

The quality of life and well-being of people living in megacities must be taken into account. Ensuring access to adequate housing, high-quality health services, green spaces, cultural and recreational activities, as well as fostering a sense of belonging and community are other challenges to be faced. In megacities, where the fast pace of life and social isolation can lead to mental health problems, promoting mental and emotional well-being is also a growing concern.

To overcome the obstacles that urbanization and megacities face, collaborative and integrated approaches are needed. As more people move to cities, it is necessary to address environmental challenges, reduce social inequalities, promote effective urban management, improve mobility and ensure better living conditions for all.

Growth of Urban Areas

◆ Challenges and opportunities in a changing world:

Population growth and migration from rural areas to urban centers are linked to the growth of urban areas. Cities expand to meet people's demand for better job opportunities, education and quality of life. However, an uncontrolled increase in population can overwhelm available resources and cause problems such as housing shortages, inadequate infrastructure and pressure on public services.

Ensuring sustainable urban planning is a major challenge for the growth of urban areas. This means encouraging balanced development that takes into account things like efficient land use, adequate infrastructure, efficient public transport, green areas, solid waste management and sustainable energy. To build resilient cities capable of dealing with problems such as climate change and the loss of natural resources, sustainable urban planning is necessary.

The growth of urban areas offers a chance to improve people's quality of life, as long as it is accompanied by policies that promote social inclusion and equality. Ensuring access to adequate housing, higher education, health services, leisure, culture and public spaces for all residents is essential.

Urban population growth demands efficient transport and mobility solutions. To reduce dependence on cars and reduce problems such as congestion and air pollution, it is necessary to plan integrated public transport systems, pedestrian and cyclist infrastructure and traffic management strategies. Sustainable mobility improves people's quality of life, reduces greenhouse gas emissions and improves public health.

Urban growth must not harm the environment. Natural resources, biodiversity and reducing the ecological footprint must be preserved in urban planning and construction. The sustainability of cities depends on the promotion of sustainable buildings, efficient use of water and proper waste management.

The growth of cities brings challenges and opportunities. It is necessary to address issues such as environmental preservation, social inclusion, quality of life, mobility and sustainable urban planning to build livable and sustainable cities.

Problems and Opportunities of Megacities

◆ A look at the challenges of the urban world:

Megacities face a number of complex challenges as global urbanization accelerates. These challenges range from providing basic services to managing limited resources. However, there are also opportunities to improve quality of life, economic growth and creativity. This text will discuss the problems and opportunities that arise from megacities.

The need for sufficient infrastructure to serve the growing population is a major challenge facing megacities. The construction of housing, schools, hospitals, transport networks, water supply and basic sanitation is a complicated and expensive task. Problems such as traffic congestion, lack of access to basic services and environmental degradation can be caused by the lack of adequate infrastructure.

The expansion of megacities has the potential to increase social disparities. Economic disparities, spatial segregation and unequal access to basic services increase with population growth. It is imperative that pressing issues such as the lack of affordable housing, sufficient jobs and adequate social services are addressed. Social tensions, instability and exclusion of marginalized groups can be caused by social inequality.

Megacities need significant natural resources such as energy, water and food. The increasing demand for these resources causes resources to be depleted, air and water pollution and loss of biodiversity to occur. To ensure the sustainability of megacities and reduce adverse environmental impacts, the sustainable management of natural resources is essential.

Congested traffic, air pollution and lack of efficient mobility are all results of the increasing number of vehicles in megacities. Overreliance on private vehicles, insufficient infrastructure for pedestrians and cyclists, and inadequate public transport are common problems. Large cities must invest in efficient public transport systems, promote the use of sustainable transport and implement smart mobility policies to improve quality of life and reduce environmental impact.

Megacities offer challenges, but also opportunities for growth and innovation. These urban centers concentrate a large amount of resources and people, making them ideal places for job creation, startups and creative industries. Megacities are also places of cultural diversity, which facilitates the exchange of knowledge and cultural enrichment.

Technology is essential to solving the problems of megacities. Improving the efficiency and quality of life in megacities can be achieved by smart solutions, such as the use of renewable energy, the digitization of public services and the adoption of data-based traffic management systems.

Citizen participation and good governance are essential to address the challenges of megacities. To ensure that policies and projects are inclusive and meet the needs of the population, the active involvement of citizens in decision-making, transparency and accountability of local governments are essential.

Megacities are complicated and difficult places where rapid population growth can cause social, economic and infrastructure problems. But these cities also offer opportunities for innovation, economic growth and improved quality of life. It is possible to build more sustainable, inclusive and resilient urban centers by addressing the problems of megacities and taking advantage of the opportunities they offer.

Sustainable Urban Planning

◆ Building cities for the future:

The aim of sustainable urban planning is to find integrated solutions that improve quality of life, environmental balance and economic growth. It is an approach that takes into account the relationships between the social, economic and environmental aspects of cities, with the aim of making urban environments healthier, fairer and more resilient.

A focus on people is fundamental in sustainable urban planning. That means prioritizing urban locations that are accessible, safe and pleasant for pedestrians and cyclists. Urban design must take into account the construction of bicycle lanes, green areas, squares, sidewalks and public spaces that foster social interaction and community well-being.

The responsible and economical use of natural resources is essential for urban sustainability. This includes using renewable energy, promoting recycling and proper waste management, and conserving water. Planning should promote sustainable practices in construction, transport and urban infrastructure.

Sustainable city planning depends on transportation. A sustainable city prioritizes efficient public transport, promoting bicycle use and establishing safe pedestrian networks. Furthermore, reducing air pollution and congestion in cities depends on approaches to traffic management and reducing reliance on private vehicles.

Green areas are essential to reduce environmental effects and improve the quality of life in cities. Sustainable urban planning prioritizes the preservation of existing natural areas, such as parks and reserves, while creating new green spaces. In addition to providing citizens with opportunities for leisure and recreation, these sites promote biodiversity, improve air quality and reduce noise.

The promotion of social equity is an essential component of sustainable urban planning. This means ensuring that everyone has equal access to basic services such as housing, education, healthcare and transport. To avoid segregation and promote social inclusion, planning must take into account social and economic diversity.

Sustainable urban planning requires active community participation. It is critical that citizens participate in the decision-making process, allowing them to express their needs and concerns. Community participation strengthens local democracy and helps build cities that respond to citizens' needs and desires.

To meet the challenges of contemporary cities and build a sustainable future, sustainable urban planning is a key approach. To make cities fairer, more resilient and healthier, it is necessary to combine social, economic and environmental elements. Sustainable urban planning requires community participation, a long-term view and cooperation between governments, the private sector and civil society.

Urban Inequality and its Social Impacts

◆ Building fairer and more inclusive cities:

The unequal distribution of resources, opportunities and basic services among different social groups within urban areas is known as urban inequality. Income, access to education, health, adequate housing, transport, security and political participation are some of the ways in which it can be seen. Urban inequality is a manifestation of the social and economic disparities that exist throughout society.

A variety of intricate factors affect urban inequality. Real estate speculation, residential segregation, racial and gender discrimination, the lack of inclusive public policies and inequalities in access to education and employment are the main causes. These elements help to perpetuate and increase social disparities in cities.

Social cohesion and people's lives are affected by urban inequality. It causes some groups to be excluded and marginalized, increasing social vulnerability and impairing the quality of life. Social inequalities increase when people do not have access to basic services such as high-quality education, adequate health and decent housing. It also limits opportunities for individual and collective growth.

The increase in crime and violence in cities is also related to urban inequality. Lack of opportunities and social exclusion can lead to areas of high crime and the marginalization of some groups, which leads to an uncontrolled cycle of poverty and violence. It is essential to implement integrated approaches that address the structural factors that contribute to inequality and security and social justice issues.

People's quality of life is directly impacted by urban inequality. The living conditions of vulnerable people are adversely affected by the lack of access to adequate medical services, clean water and basic sanitation. In addition, exposure to polluted environments, lack of green space and poor housing conditions contribute to the emergence of diseases and increase morbidity and mortality rates.

Solving urban inequality requires a multifaceted and comprehensive approach. In addition to taking measures to reduce discrimination and residential segregation, it is necessary to finance inclusive public policies that encourage the equitable distribution of resources and services. To ensure that policies are effective and meet the needs of communities, it is necessary to increase citizen participation and civil society involvement.

To make cities more equitable, sustainable and welcoming for all, governments, civic organizations and the private sector must work together to tackle urban inequality. We can transform our cities into spaces where all people have the opportunity to live in dignity and reach their full potential through raising awareness and implementing inclusive policies and practices.

Future perspectives

◆ Shaping the fate of the world's population:

The continued growth of the world's population is one of the most important prospects for the future. Although the rate of global population growth has slowed in recent decades, the world's population is still growing. By 2050, it is estimated that the population will reach 9.7 billion people. This will pose major hurdles with regard to food supply, housing, health and environmental sustainability.

Population aging is another important perspective. People are living longer due to improvements in quality of life and health, which increases the proportion of elderly people in the population. Due to the aging of the population, there are problems in sectors such as health care, social security and adapting cities to meet the needs of the elderly.

Migration and diversity are also linked to the future prospects of the population. The demographic composition of societies continues to be influenced by migration, both internal and external. The growing diversity of cultural, religious and ethnic backgrounds has a significant impact on social cohesion, the economy and the formulation of public policies.

Another important perspective for the future is the trend towards urbanization. A growing number of individuals are migrating to urban areas in search of job opportunities, higher education and access to public services. The rapid growth of cities causes problems in infrastructure, housing, transport and quality of life. But it also offers opportunities for smarter, more sustainable and inclusive cities.

The world's population will be impacted by the rapid evolution of automation and technology. Automation, artificial intelligence and robotics have the potential to change the economy, society and the workforce. Changes like these can pave the way for new job opportunities, but they also require continuous learning and adaptation for people to be prepared for work in the future.

Sustainability and climate change are closely linked to the future prospects of the world's population. Adopting sustainable practices in terms of energy, land use, waste management and ecosystem conservation is essential as populations grow and demand for resources increases. To ensure a livable future for future generations, mitigating and adapting to climate change are crucial challenges.

We are clearly facing a variety of complicated obstacles as well as significant opportunities. It is critical that governments, international organizations, the private sector and civil society collaborate to address issues such as population growth, aging, migration, urbanization, sustainability, technology and climate change to create a prosperous and sustainable future.

Population-Ageing

◆ The Longevity Revolution:

The aging of the world's population is a worldwide phenomenon never seen before in recent centuries. Factors such as advances in medicine, improvements in living conditions, access to health care and changes in family structures contribute to this phenomenon. The proportion of elderly people in the total population is growing rapidly as life expectancy increases.

There are several factors that contribute to an aging population. One of the main factors is the declining fertility rate, which means fewer children are being born to replace the elderly. In addition, medical advances have increased longevity and reduced mortality in various age groups.

Population aging has several significant social and economic effects. There are changes in family structures at the social level, with fewer multigenerational families and more elderly people living alone or in long-term care facilities. This affects family life, loneliness and the need for adequate senior support systems.

In economic terms, the aging of the population puts the sustainability of social security and health systems at risk. Resources devoted to pension benefits and health care are under pressure due to the higher proportion of older people in relation to the working-age population. It is essential to reassess social protection systems and create plans to ensure long-term financial sustainability.

The longevity revolution has led to the need for proper health care for the elderly. With the increase in life expectancy, it is necessary to encourage healthy and active aging. This can be achieved through access to high-quality medical services, prevention and health promotion programs and specialist care for age-related diseases and disabilities.

While an aging population presents challenges, there are also opportunities to be explored. The knowledge and experience accumulated by seniors can be used to foster creativity, innovation and economic growth. Furthermore, a society that values age diversity and provides opportunities for people of all ages makes things more inclusive and fair.

Population aging is an inevitable reality, but it also offers the opportunity to redefine concepts, policies and practices related to aging and longevity. It is imperative to create plans to promote healthy aging, ensure the sustainability of social protection and health systems and build a society that respects and values all age groups.

Global Aging Trends

◆ The aging of the global population:

Population aging is a global reality. The number of people over 60 is increasing in all regions of the world, according to the data. In developed countries, where life expectancy is higher and the fertility rate is lower, this growth is particularly marked. However, due to the demographic transition and increasing life expectancy, the population of developing countries is aging rapidly.

The world's population ages for a variety of reasons. The main factor is the decrease in the fertility rate, which is caused by changes in social standards, greater access to education and contraceptives, as well as the entry of women into the labor market. In addition, more people are reaching old age as a result of advances in health and medicine.

Population aging affects many aspects of society. There are changes in family structures at the social level, with fewer multigenerational families and more elderly people living alone. This can result in more social isolation and the need for adequate support systems for seniors. Furthermore, social roles and intergenerational relationships may change as a result of an aging population.

Population aging affects social security and health systems in economic terms. The contributor base to social security systems has shrunk and the demand for health care has risen due to the higher ratio of older people to the working-age population. For these systems to be sustainable, they need to be reviewed and adapted.

While population aging presents challenges, it also presents opportunities. It is essential that societies take a comprehensive approach to addressing these challenges, taking into account policies that promote healthy ageing, the well-being of the elderly and social inclusion. In addition, population aging can be an occasion to rethink conventional concepts of productivity, retirement and work, giving older people the chance to contribute to society.

The impact on the health and well-being of the elderly is an important component of population aging. Policies and programs that promote healthy aging, with access to high-quality health care, long-term care and person-centered approaches, must keep pace with increasing life expectancy. The problems of the elderly, such as dementia, reduced mobility and chronic diseases, require investments in research and interventions.

Societies must prepare to face the obstacles and take advantage of the opportunities that population aging brings. To build a sustainable and equitable society, it is necessary to implement policies and programs that encourage the inclusion, health and well-being of the elderly. As a writer, I hope this text will raise awareness and debate about global aging trends and inspire positive action for a future where all generations can live in dignity and prosperity.

Ageing Population

◆ Contributing factors:

The advancement of medicine and health care is one of the main causes of population aging. Living conditions and access to medical services have improved significantly in recent decades. This has led to longer life expectancy, lower infant mortality and lower overall death rates. In addition, new treatments, drugs and medical technologies have increased life expectancy.

Population aging is strongly influenced by socioeconomic changes. The agricultural economy moves into the industrialized economy as societies grow economically. Work patterns, urbanization and access to education change with the transition. The fertility rate tends to decrease with increasing urbanization, while life expectancy increases due to better living conditions and access to health care.

One of the main factors contributing to the aging of the population is the decline in the fertility rate. Due to changes in societal values, greater access to education and work opportunities for women, as well as family planning measures, families in many countries are choosing to have fewer children. The proportion of elderly people in the population increases when fewer children are born.

Migration and urbanization play a significant role in aging populations. Demographic patterns change as people migrate to cities in search of financial opportunities. Rural areas have more young people, while urban areas have more elderly people. This is partly due to the fact that many young people migrate to cities in search of work, while the elderly tend to remain in their home areas.

In addition to the fertility rate, other fertility-related factors may affect population aging. This encompasses issues such as infertility, postponing the age of childbearing, and personal decision not to have children. The average age of mothers and fathers increases as people delay motherhood and fatherhood for personal, professional or financial reasons. This can affect the fertility rate and therefore the aging of the population.

Due to a series of interdependent factors, population aging is a complex and multifaceted phenomenon. This is heavily influenced by socioeconomic changes, migration and urbanization, falling fertility rates, advances in medicine and health care, and fertility-related issues.

Social and Economic Implications of Aging

◆ Changes in family structures:

Family structures are significantly affected by an aging population. As people live longer, they are more likely to have fewer or no children at all. This leads to smaller families and more elderly people living alone. These changes require a reorganization of family dynamics and can have an impact on support and care for the elderly.

The aging of the population also brings health problems. The demand for specialized medical services, such as treatments for chronic illnesses, palliative care and long-term care, increases with an aging population. Growing demand can overwhelm health systems, requiring investments and policies to ensure that health services are of good quality and accessible to the elderly population.

In the economic context, the aging of the population affects the labor market. As people live longer, many choose to continue working past retirement age. This can result in job shortages for young people and the need for programs to re-skill and adapt the skills of older workers. In addition, companies can benefit from the knowledge and experience accumulated by older employees.

Population aging puts pension systems at risk. With more people retired and a smaller proportion of active workers contributing to these systems, financial sustainability is becoming more of a concern. This requires changes in pension systems, such as raising the retirement age, introducing supplementary pension plans, and encouraging active aging sond extended working lives.

In addition to obstacles, an aging population offers opportunities for economic growth. Specific sectors of the economy can be driven by increased demand for products and services aimed at the elderly, such as adapted housing, assistive technologies and leisure. The experience and knowledge of seniors can also be used to foster entrepreneurship and innovation.

Population aging has significant economic and social consequences. It is essential that governments, organizations and society in general are prepared to deal with the difficulties and take advantage of the opportunities that arise with this demographic change. A successful transition to a world with an aging population depends on investments in health care, policies for inclusion in the labor market, reforms in social security systems and recognition of the economic potential of the elderly.

Public Policies for the Elderly

◆ Care:

Improving access to and quality of health services is a critical public policy for the care of the elderly. It is critical that older people have access to preventive care, specialist treatments and affordable medicines. In addition, priority should be given to disease prevention programs, screening for health conditions, and rehabilitation services. In such a situation, significant measures are taken to strengthen health systems and train professionals to address the specific needs of older people.

Ensuring that the elderly have adequate housing is essential for their well-being and quality of life. Public policies that increase physical and financial accessibility, such as subsidy programs and the construction of adapted housing, are essential. In addition, it is essential to promote community aging, offering spaces and services to support the elderly, such as accessible public transport and opportunities for social involvement.

It is necessary to create long-term care policies to meet the needs of elderly people who need daily or specialized care, given the increase in life expectancy. These services can range from home care to institutional care. An integrated system that offers physical, emotional and social support to the elderly and their families must be created, including respite programs and support for caregivers.

Violence and abuse of the elderly must be combated by public policies. This includes legislation and regulations to protect older people, raise awareness of the issue and provide support and reporting services. Furthermore, the training of justice agents, social workers and health professionals is crucial to identify and adequately respond to incidents of abuse and violence.

Social inclusion and the active participation of the elderly are critical for the quality of life and well-being of individuals. Opportunities for lifelong learning, recreational activities, volunteerism and civic involvement should be promoted by public policy. In addition, it is essential to establish places and initiatives that value the experience and knowledge of the elderly, helping to prevent social isolation and promoting intergenerational interaction.

Public policies for the care of the elderly are essential to ensure that this population lives a dignified life, with access to adequate health services, adequate housing, long-term care, protection against violence and abuse, and opportunities to actively participate in society. It is imperative that governments, organizations and society at large commit to the development and implementation of these policies as population aging becomes a global reality. We will build a fairer and more inclusive society for all through the care and appreciation of the elderly.

New Challenges and Solutions

◆ Climate change and sustainability:

The impact of climate change and the need for sustainable solutions is one of the most pressing issues we face. Rising greenhouse gas emissions, environmental degradation and scarcity of natural resources require urgent action. To reduce the effects of climate change and ensure a sustainable future for future generations, methods such as the transition to renewable energy, the development of clean technologies, the promotion of the circular economy and awareness of sustainable consumption are needed.

The rapid development of technologies such as robotics, automation and artificial intelligence brings both challenges and opportunities. While automation can result in job losses, it also offers the opportunity to improve quality of life and efficiency. It is necessary to invest in education and professional requalification programs to prepare people for the jobs of the future. Furthermore, to avoid social exclusion, digital inclusion policies and equal access to technology are essential.

In many parts of the world, social and economic inequality persists. It is necessary to implement policies that reduce income disparity, guarantee equal access to education, health and economic opportunities, combat discrimination and promote social inclusion to solve this problem. Reducing inequality and building fairer societies can be achieved through measures such as income transfer programs, policies that promote gender equality, investments in infrastructure and incentives for entrepreneurship.

Population aging is a worldwide phenomenon that presents both problems and opportunities. It is critical to create policies and services that meet the needs of older people, such as adequate health care, adapted housing and opportunities for social participation, as life expectancy increases. In addition, it is imperative to reevaluate retirement policies and promote active aging, respecting the knowledge and experience of the elderly.

Cultural diversity, social integration and the management of migratory flows are issues faced by globalization and migration. It is critical to support policies that enable inclusion, combat racial discrimination and help migrants integrate into their new communities. In addition, to ensure respect for human rights and address the challenges of migration, international cooperation and the search for global solutions are necessary.

Health and Well-Being of the Population

◆ Investing in our greatest asset:

Health is fundamental to human advancement. A healthy population increases productivity, reduces poverty and improves quality of life. As a result, it is imperative that governments, international organizations and society in general recognize health as a priority and invest in policies and programs that improve the well-being of the population.

Ensuring that everyone has access to health services is a major challenge. Basic healthcare is difficult to obtain in many countries, especially those with low incomes. It is critical that health policies are implemented to ensure that everyone has equal access to health services such as primary care, prevention, treatment and long-term care.

To reduce the burden on health systems, it is necessary to invest in health promotion and disease prevention. Disease prevention and well-being promotion can be achieved through health education, awareness of healthy habits, vaccination and adoption of healthy lifestyles. In addition, it is essential to invest in research and development of new therapies and technologies that help prevent and treat diseases.

Population health faces difficult and ever-changing problems. Antimicrobial resistance, global epidemics, public health emergencies and the rise of chronic diseases require rapid and effective responses. Health systems must have the capacity to deal with these problems by investing in infrastructure, training health professionals and implementing epidemiological surveillance systems.

The mental and emotional health of the population is vital in addition to physical health. People's quality of life is significantly affected by problems such as stress, anxiety and depression. Funds are needed to promote mental health, ensure access to high-quality mental health care, and raise awareness of the need for psychological care.

One of the best investments a society can make is to invest in the health and well-being of its population. A healthy population is more productive, more resilient and better able to deal with the difficulties of the modern world. We can promote health and well-being broadly and fairly through appropriate public policy, sustainable financing, scientific research and international cooperation.

Access to Health Services

A universal right to health and well-being:

A person's ability to seek and receive medical treatment when needed is known as access to health services. Access to health, medication, exams, vaccination, treatment and disease prevention are examples of this. Universal access to health services is essential for prompt diagnosis and appropriate treatment of medical conditions, which improves people's quality of life and reduces the effect that disease has on them.

The main objective of the World Health Organization (WHO) is to ensure that health is accessible to all. This means that everyone should have access to essential health services, regardless of socioeconomic status, place of residence, gender or age. Universal access is essential to ensure that everyone has the opportunity to achieve the best possible level of health.

While universal access to health care is a desirable goal, there are several obstacles that prevent this goal from being fully achieved. In many parts of the world, especially in low-income countries, poverty, lack of health infrastructure, lack of qualified health professionals and a shortage of health professionals are significant obstacles to adequate access to medical services. Furthermore, marginalized groups such as people with disabilities, ethnic minorities and rural populations may face additional problems accessing health services.

The cost of medical care is one of the main barriers to accessing health services. Low-income people may not have access to essential medical care due to the health care system, which in many countries is based on out-of-pocket payments. In addition, lack of coverage or lack of health insurance can be significant obstacles. Implementing appropriate financing policies, such as insurance-based health systems or tax-funded public health systems, is essential to overcome these obstacles.

Regional inequality is an additional barrier to accessing health services. In many countries, rural populations have limited access to medical care due to the concentration of health services in urban areas. This can result in significant differences in health between rural and urban people. It is necessary to work together to ensure high quality health services in all areas, including remote and hard to reach places.

There are several ways to increase access to health services. Adequate healthcare infrastructure should be prioritized, including building hospitals, clinics and health centers in remote and underdeveloped locations. In addition, there is a need to train and train a sufficient number of health professionals to ensure that doctors, nurses and other qualified professionals are available in all regions.

Health education and preventive health promotion are other important strategies. This includes raising awareness about healthy habits, vaccination and disease prevention. Promoting healthy lifestyles and preventing disease can improve the health of the population as a whole and reduce the need for intensive medical care.

Improved access to health services can be achieved through effective public policies. Implementing inclusive health systems, such as universal health insurance or health programs for low-income people, is part of this. Furthermore, it is crucial to address health inequalities through policies that take into account the unique requirements of marginalized groups.

A fundamental and essential human right for the well-being of societies and individuals is access to health services. Broad and collaborative work between governments, international organizations, health professionals and society in general is needed to overcome barriers to access to health.

To ensure that everyone has access to the health services they need, it is necessary to invest in health infrastructure, train health professionals, promote preventive health and implement adequate public policies.

Global Public Health Challenges

◆ Addressing threats to human health:

Health emergencies, which spread rapidly, are a major concern in global public health. Pandemics, epidemics, outbreaks of infectious diseases and biological threats are major difficulties. Recent examples include the COVID-19 pandemic, the spread of the Zika virus, and the threat of diseases such as Ebola. There is a need for governments, communities and international health organizations to respond to these emergencies in a swift and coordinated manner.

The other major problem for global public health is antimicrobial resistance. The overuse and misuse of antibiotics has caused drug-resistant bacteria to proliferate, making it more difficult to treat common infections. This jeopardizes the medical advances achieved over decades and puts the effectiveness of treatments at risk. A multifaceted approach is needed to address antimicrobial resistance, including regulating the use of antibiotics, educating on their proper use, and researching and developing new drugs.

Global public health is facing a growing challenge from chronic non-communicable diseases such as diabetes, heart disease, cancer and chronic respiratory diseases. A significant number of deaths and the quality of life of millions of people are caused by these diseases. The increase in these diseases is caused by risk factors such as smoking, excessive alcohol consumption, poor diet and lack of physical activity. To reduce the incidence and effects of chronic non-communicable diseases, preventive measures, health promotion and access to adequate treatments are necessary.

In global public health, health inequality persists. People who are marginalized, such as the poor, ethnic minorities, migrants and refugees, are more likely to contract disease and have less access to high-quality health care. A comprehensive approach is needed to reduce health inequalities, which includes social, political and financial actions to improve access to health services, combat discrimination and address the social determinants of health.

Global public health is heavily affected by climate change. Rising temperatures, extreme weather events, and environmental degradation increase the incidence of vector-borne diseases such as malaria and dengue, in addition to increasing the prevalence of respiratory and cardiovascular diseases. It is necessary to implement climate change mitigation measures and increase the adaptive capacity of communities to deal with the health impacts of dealing with this problem.

Public health issues around the world are complicated and require an integrated and comprehensive approach. Investing in research, health infrastructure and efficient surveillance systems are needed. In addition, international cooperation and knowledge exchange are essential to share good practices and respond to health emergencies.

Epidemiology and Disease Prevention

Safeguarding global health:
Epidemiology is a field that studies how diseases appear and spread in the population and any factors that influence them. Epidemiologists collect and analyze data to find patterns and trends, identify risk factors, and provide important information for public health decision-making. Epidemiology helps to better understand diseases, find risk groups and establish more effective preventive interventions.

Epidemiological surveillance is vital for the early detection and control of diseases. Health professionals can monitor disease incidence and prevalence, identify outbreaks, and take appropriate control measures through systematic data collection. Epidemiological surveillance also helps prevent epidemics and pandemics by identifying new diseases and responding quickly to public health threats.

Primary prevention involves disease prevention. Health promotion and risk factor reduction are examples of this. In prevention, several strategies are used, including health education programs, vaccination policies, awareness campaigns on healthy lifestyles and environmental control. Primary prevention aims to create healthy environments and encourage people to make healthy choices by addressing the social, environmental and behavioral determinants of health.

Secondary prevention aims to identify diseases in their early stages, when they can still be treated most successfully. Secondary prevention interventions include screening tests such as mammograms, colonoscopies and blood tests. Early detection allows prompt treatment, reducing disease progression and increasing survival rates.

In addition, monitoring high-risk populations and taking specific preventive measures are examples of secondary prevention.

Tertiary prevention aims to reduce complications and improve the quality of life for individuals already suffering from a persistent or disabling illness. Proper disease management, rehabilitation, palliative care, and emotional support are among these things. Tertiary prevention aims to reduce the consequences of the disease, help people become more independent and improve their quality of life.

Despite major advances in disease epidemiology and prevention, we still face major obstacles. We need to overcome challenges such as globalization, demographic changes and inadequate health systems. Furthermore, the COVID-19 pandemic has shown how important adequate preparedness for health emergencies is and how important it is to strengthen monitoring and response systems.

However, there are also chances to improve disease prevention. New avenues for disease surveillance and treatment have been opened up by technological advances such as telemedicine and artificial intelligence. In addition, to face global health challenges, it is essential that countries, international organizations and sectors of society collaborate, promoting the exchange of resources and knowledge.

Epidemiology and disease prevention are important to promote global health. We can improve the quality of life for people around the world by studying the patterns and causes of disease and adopting effective prevention methods.

Medical Advances and Their Implications

◆ Transforming health and society:

The ability to make more accurate and personalized diagnoses is one of the most remarkable advances in modern medicine. Doctors can identify diseases at early stages using sophisticated imaging techniques, genetic testing and biomarkers. Precision medicine also allows treatments to be tailored to each patient's genetic and individual characteristics, which results in better results and fewer side effects.

Regenerative medicine and gene therapy have the potential to revolutionize the treatment of degenerative and genetic diseases. Gene therapy consists of inserting healthy genetic material into diseased cells to correct the genetic mutations that cause the disease. Regenerative medicine, on the other hand, regenerates damaged tissues or organs using stem cells and other methods. These advances can cure diseases that were previously considered impossible to cure.

In the medical field, machine learning and artificial intelligence (AI) have shown promise. Advanced algorithms can analyze vast amounts of medical data, helping doctors quickly diagnose illnesses, create personalized treatments and predict clinical outcomes. AI can also help perform robot-assisted surgeries more accurately and with less risk. It is important to think about ethical issues and ensure that the benefits of AI are distributed fairly.

Digital health and telemedicine can make healthcare more accessible and convenient. People can receive medical care without the need for physical travel through health apps, patient monitoring and remote consultations. This is particularly advantageous for rural locations and where health services are difficult to obtain. However, healthcare professionals need to be trained to use these technologies effectively, as well as ensuring that patient data is secure.

Medical advances raise significant moral and social issues. For example, while gene editing is a promising method, there are questions about the ethical consequences of altering human DNA. Furthermore, the availability of sophisticated and expensive treatments can increase disparities in access to healthcare, widening the gap between those who can afford these innovations and those who cannot. It is imperative that research and implementation of medical advances be conducted ethically, considering social, economic and ethical effects.

Promotion of Well-Being and Quality of Life

◆ The path to a fulfilling life:

Well-being and quality of life depend on physical health. To keep our bodies healthy, it is important to follow a healthy lifestyle, which includes healthy eating, regular exercise and adequate sleep. In addition, maintaining good physical health requires regular visits to the doctor and seeking treatments and disease prevention.

Our quality of life depends on our mental and emotional health. To maintain emotional balance and resilience, it is essential to take care of our mental health. This can be achieved through activities such as meditation, yoga, self-care and therapy. It is essential to create a culture that is supportive and understanding, where mental health is considered and treated equally with physical health.

Healthy relationships are essential for quality of life and well-being. Building meaningful bonds with friends, family, and community gives us a sense of emotional belonging and belonging. To live a full and happy life, you must invest time and energy in quality relationships, listen and be heard, cultivate emotional bonds and build support networks.

An essential component of well-being is having a sense of purpose and meaning in our lives. By discovering activities that bring us personal satisfaction and that are in line with our values and interests, we can feel more motivated and feel that we are doing what we want. This could include work, volunteer activities, personal interests or personal projects. To improve well-being and quality of life, it is necessary to balance our daily responsibilities with our personal passions.

These days, finding a healthy balance between work and personal life is difficult. Lack of time, stress and work overload can harm our health and well-being. It is critical to set healthy boundaries, set priorities, assign tasks when possible, and make time for recreation, rest, and relaxation.

Where we live also impacts our quality of life. Our physical and mental well-being is enhanced by a clean, safe and sustainable environment. To ensure a healthy environment for both ourselves and future generations, we can care for our environment, reduce our ecological footprint, have access to green spaces and promote sustainable practices.

To live a happy and fulfilling life, you must continually learn and develop. Learning, whether through courses, reading, travel or experiences, helps us broaden our horizons, develop new skills and grow as individuals. The quest for knowledge keeps us curious, engaged and receptive to new perspectives.

Improving quality of life and well-being is a personal and continuous journey. It takes care of our physical, mental and emotional health, cultivating meaningful relationships, finding purpose and meaning in our lives, finding a balance between our work and personal lives, establishing a healthy environment and continuing to learn and grow.

Population and Environment

The importance of sustainability:

One of the main factors affecting the environment is population growth. Demand for natural resources such as water, food, energy and land is increasing as the world's population continues to increase. This puts pressure on ecosystems and can cause environmental degradation, loss of resources and loss of biodiversity.

In addition to population growth, unsustainable lifestyle patterns and excessive consumption are other factors contributing to environmental pressures. The excessive consumption of goods and services in developed countries, in particular, leads to the overexploitation of natural resources and the production of a large amount of waste. It is imperative to reassess our consumption practices and seek more sustainable lifestyles, putting preservation and the economical use of resources in the first place.

Human activities are directly responsible for the increase in greenhouse gas emissions and climate change. Some of the main causes of climate change include intensive agriculture, deforestation and the burning of fossil fuels. Melting glaciers, rising sea levels, the intensification of extreme weather events and changing weather patterns are some of the significant impacts of these changes on the environment. It is imperative to take immediate action to reduce greenhouse gas emissions and minimize the effects of climate change.

For the health of ecosystems and the survival of all forms of life on the planet, the preservation of biodiversity is fundamental. Biodiversity is rapidly being lost around the world as a result of urban sprawl, pollution, destruction of natural habitats and overexploitation of resources. To preserve life on Earth, it is essential to protect natural areas, adopt sustainable agricultural techniques and raise awareness of biodiversity.

Faced with these obstacles, the pursuit of sustainability is essential. That means finding ways to balance human development and environmental preservation. The adoption of renewable energy sources, the promotion of energy efficiency, the responsible use of natural resources, sustainable agriculture, sustainable transport and environmental education are sustainable solutions.

A collective approach is needed to address population and environmental issues on a global scale. Governments, non-governmental organizations, businesses and individuals can help promote sustainable practices. Furthermore, to address global challenges and create a sustainable future for all, international cooperation and knowledge sharing are essential.

The relationship between the population and their environment is complicated and difficult to understand. Taking action to preserve our planet is essential as the world's population continues to increase. The main objective must be sustainability, which aims to balance human development with the preservation of natural resources and conservation of biodiversity.

Population Pressures on Natural Resources

◆ Challenges and solutions:

Population growth has a direct impact on the demand for natural resources such as water, food, energy and materials. The pressure on these resources increases exponentially as more people enter the picture. For example, rising demand for food leads to more deforestation for agricultural expansion, excessive use of pesticides and fertilizers, and excessive irrigation. These actions have a significant impact on biodiversity and natural ecosystems.

Human life and ecosystems depend on water. But the growing demand for clean water for agriculture, industry and power generation has caused water shortages in many parts of the world. Furthermore, the problem is compounded by water pollution. To face the challenges of water scarcity, it is essential to adopt sustainable water management practices, such as conservation, reuse and investment in water infrastructure.

The task of increasing food production to feed an expanding population is a complicated challenge. Soil degradation, nutrient depletion and loss of biodiversity can result from agricultural expansion and production intensification. Furthermore, extreme weather events and changes in rainfall patterns are other problems caused by climate change. To maintain food security, it is necessary to adopt sustainable agricultural practices, invest in efficient production technologies and promote a healthy and sustainable diet.

Depletion of natural resources such as fossil fuels, minerals and forests is occurring due to the unsustainable use of these resources.

Biodiversity loss, soil degradation and environmental pollution are the result of over-extraction of natural resources without proper management. It is essential to adopt a more conscious approach to natural resources that encourages conservation, economical use, investment in renewable energy and the transition to a circular economy.

Climate change is directly linked to rising greenhouse gas emissions and population growth. Some of the main causes of greenhouse gas emissions include deforestation, intensive agriculture and the burning of fossil fuels to produce energy. Water availability, weather patterns, food security and biodiversity are all affected by climate change. Reducing carbon emissions and transitioning to clean energy sources are necessary mitigation measures to address this issue.

Solutions: Information and Awareness:

Raising awareness of the importance of sustainability and the effects of population growth on natural resources depends on education. Increasing public awareness of sustainable practices can result in more conscientious actions and lifestyles.

Family Planning: It is necessary for everyone to have access to family planning services so that they can have as many children as they want. This reduces pressure on natural resources and helps to control population growth.

Sustainable Use of Natural Resources: The conservation of natural resources and the reduction of waste are fundamental to the adoption of sustainable practices in agriculture, fisheries, forestry and industry.

Renewable Energy and Energy Efficiency: The shift to clean energy sources such as solar, wind and hydropower is essential to reduce greenhouse gas emissions and minimize the effects of climate change.

Conservation of Biodiversity: To preserve the natural wealth of our planet, it is essential to protect ecosystems and biodiversity. The establishment of protected areas and the construction of ecological corridors are crucial strategies in this regard.

The pressures that the population exerts on natural resources constitute an urgent challenge that requires immediate measures. As a writer, my duty is to inform and inspire people to take sustainable action and support policies that promote the conservation of natural resources.

Climate Change and Population Impacts

◆ Challenges and solutions:
One of the main consequences of climate change is the increase in average global temperature. Excessive heat damages people's health, especially vulnerable groups such as children and the elderly. In addition, extreme weather phenomena such as hurricanes, floods and droughts are becoming more common and severe, causing deaths, damage to infrastructure and displacement of people.

Food production and water availability are highly affected by climate change. Food shortages are caused by prolonged droughts and erratic rainfall, which affect agriculture and lower crop productivity. In addition, rising sea levels and infiltration of salt water into groundwater can contaminate freshwater sources, further aggravating the situation of water scarcity in many parts of the world.

Human health is also heavily impacted by climate change. Rising temperatures and the proliferation of vectors such as mosquitoes and ticks contribute to the spread of climate-borne diseases such as malaria, dengue, Zika and heat-related illnesses. These diseases are more common among vulnerable populations, especially those with limited access to health services.

The world's population is changing due to climate change. Entire communities are fleeing their homes in search of safer places due to rising sea levels, floods, prolonged droughts and extreme weather events. Humanitarian crises, conflicts and pressure on resources in receiving areas can result from this population displacement.

Solutions to reduce greenhouse gas emissions include:

Reducing greenhouse gas emissions is critical to limiting global warming and mitigating the effects of climate change. The transition to renewable energy sources, investments in energy efficiency, energy conservation and reforestation measures are significant steps in this direction.

Adaptation and Resilience: Communities must learn to adapt and adapt to climate change. Investments in agriculture and water management that take into account climate variability, sustainable urban planning, early warning systems and building robust and adaptable infrastructure are all part of this.

Education and Awareness: Education and public awareness are essential to adopting sustainable practices and building a culture that is respectful of the environment. People can change their behavior and find solutions if they are informed and involved about the effects of climate change.

International Cooperation: Coordinated global efforts are needed to mitigate and adapt to climate change. To overcome this challenge, nations must work together, exchange knowledge and collaborate.

One of the greatest threats to the world's population is climate change. Its impact spans food security and water scarcity, as well as population displacement and human health. However, there are alternatives and methods that can be implemented to mitigate these consequences and build a more sustainable future. International cooperation, education, adaptation and resilience are needed to reduce greenhouse gas emissions.

Sustainability and Sustainable Development

◆ Building a balanced future:

The ability to meet the needs of the present without compromising the ability of future generations to meet their own needs is known as sustainability. It is necessary to balance the economic, social and environmental aspects of development, adopting a comprehensive and long-term perspective.

Sustainability is threatened by a series of problems that our society faces. Some examples include the depletion of natural resources, environmental degradation, poverty, social inequalities and climate change. These obstacles are linked to each other and need to be overcome through a comprehensive method.

A key concept for achieving sustainability is sustainable development. It is based on three interconnected pillars: economic, social and environmental. In order to ensure social equality, economic growth and environmental preservation, these pillars must be examined together.

To achieve sustainable development, various solutions and plans must be implemented in several areas:

Sustainable Energy: Promote the transition to renewable energy sources and increase energy efficiency to reduce greenhouse gas emissions and decrease dependence on fossil fuels.

Sustainable Use of Natural Resources: Ensure the sustainable management of natural resources, preventing depletion and degradation, and promoting conservation and recycling.

Sustainable Agriculture: Investing in sustainable agricultural practices, such as organic agriculture and agroecology, to preserve soils, biodiversity and ensure food security.

Responsible Consumption and Production: Promote sustainable consumption patterns, reduce waste, favor products and production processes with low environmental impact and value the circular economy.

Social Inclusion and Equity: Ensure that sustainable development is inclusive, promoting equal opportunities, social justice and respect for human rights.

Education and Awareness: Investing in education and awareness to create a culture of sustainability, empowering people to make informed and responsible decisions.

Necessary Actions:

To move towards sustainability and sustainable development, it is essential to adopt concrete actions:

Public Policy: Governments should implement policies that encourage sustainable practices, establish targets and regulations, and promote cooperation between the public and private sectors.

Partnerships and Cooperation: Collaboration between governments, businesses, non-governmental organizations and civil society is essential to effectively address sustainability challenges.

Innovation and Technology: Investments in research and development of clean and sustainable technologies are essential to drive the transition to a more sustainable future.

Citizen Participation: Engaging the population in decision-making, valuing the participation of civil society and encouraging individual responsibility are foundations for building a more sustainable society.

To ensure a just and prosperous future, sustainability and sustainable development are essential. As a writer, I understand the importance of spreading information and awareness about this important topic. Our obligation is to encourage reflection and action towards sustainability in all aspects of our lives, from personal decisions to global policies.

Conservation and Preservation Policies

Safeguarding the natural heritage:

To preserve natural resources and maintain ecosystem balance, preservation and conservation are fundamental. Our natural heritage provides natural resources, biodiversity and ecosystem services that are essential for human survival and well-being. In addition, natural spaces have cultural, aesthetic and intrinsic values that must be preserved for current and future generations.

Conservation and preservation policies face several obstacles. Some examples include human pressure on natural resources, habitat destruction, pollution, climate change and loss of biodiversity. In addition, political, social and economic problems can hinder the effective implementation of conservation and preservation policies.

To deal with these obstacles, efficient conservation and preservation strategies are needed:

Protected Places: The preservation of ecosystems and species depends on the creation and management of protected areas, such as national parks, nature reserves and world heritage sites. These areas are home to biodiversity and play an important role in sustainable tourism and scientific research.

Sustainable Management of Natural Resources: The sustainable use of natural resources, such as forests, oceans and water resources, requires the implementation of policies and regulations. This includes conservation agriculture, responsible fishing and sustainable forest management.

Environmental Education: The promotion of conservation and preservation depends on environmental awareness and education. In order for local communities, younger generations and decision-makers to understand the importance of protecting the environment and adopting sustainable behaviours, it is critical that they get involved.

International Cooperation: To address global conservation and preservation challenges, it is critical that countries, non-governmental organizations and international institutions work together. International agreements such as the Convention on Biological Diversity encourage collaboration and cooperation in protecting the environment.

Long-Term Implications: In addition to environmental protection, conservation and preservation policies have long-term consequences. They help with food security, human health, economic and social stability and the mitigation of global warming. Furthermore, the conservation and preservation of natural ecosystems is crucial for the resilience and adaptation of natural systems to environmental changes.

Approaches to a Sustainable Future

Building a resilient world:

To ensure a prosperous and healthy future for all forms of life that inhabit planet Earth, sustainability is a fundamental concept. Recognizing that social, economic and environmental needs are linked to each other, it tries to strike a balance between these three pillars. Sustainability depends on sustainable and fair economic practices, responsible management of natural resources and reduction of social inequalities.

It is difficult to build a sustainable future because we face several important problems. Examples include poverty, social inequality, the depletion of natural resources, climate change, environmental degradation and the growing demand for energy. These difficulties are related and require.

Fortunately, a variety of promising solutions and methods are being adopted around the world. I'm listing some of them:

Renewable Energy: Reducing greenhouse gas emissions and decreasing our dependence on fossil fuels requires a shift to clean, renewable energy sources. Investments in renewable sources such as solar, wind and hydropower are increasing and are contributing to a more sustainable future.

Circular Economy: The circular economy is an approach that aims to reduce waste and encourage the recycling, reuse and recovery of goods. We can reduce pressure on natural resources and reduce environmental effects by adopting more sustainable production and consumption practices.

Sustainable Urban Development: The goal of sustainable urban planning is to make cities greener, more compact and energy efficient. The use of public transport, the expansion of green spaces, the construction of resilient infrastructures and the formation of inclusive communities are examples of this.

Sustainable Agriculture: Sustainable agriculture prioritizes food production in an environmentally responsible way, using agricultural practices that preserve natural resources, protect biodiversity and increase food security. The implementation of organic farming methods, agroecology and the conscious use of pesticides and fertilizers are part of this.

Education and Awareness: Building a sustainable future depends on education. It is critical to raise awareness of the obstacles we face, the consequences of our choices, and the solutions available. To make people more aware of and involved in environmental issues, it is essential to invest in educational programs that encourage sustainable lifestyles and address these issues.

The contribution of public policies:

Public policies are essential to guarantee a sustainable future. It is the responsibility of governments to establish and implement regulations and incentives that encourage sustainable practices in all sectors of society. This includes setting ambitious targets to reduce emissions, implementing environmental conservation programs, promoting investment in renewable energy and fostering the circular economy.

Social Inequalities and Vulnerable Population

◆ In search of a fairer world:

The way resources, opportunities and power are distributed in a society is called social inequality. Complex factors such as poverty, discrimination, lack of access to basic services, social exclusion and lack of education and employment opportunities are often the cause of them. Social inequalities have a significant impact on all aspects of people's lives, including health and well-being and future prospects.

Social inequalities particularly affect certain population groups. Children, the elderly, people with disabilities, ethnic minorities, refugees, migrants, homeless people and vulnerable women are among these groups. These people are more vulnerable to social exclusion, poverty, violence and marginalization and face more challenges in living a dignified life.

The lack of access to essential services, such as health, education, adequate housing and clean water and basic sanitation, is one of the main forms of social inequality. While these services are essential to ensuring everyone's growth and well-being, many vulnerable groups face significant obstacles to obtaining them. Regardless of your social or economic status, it is essential to ensure that these services are accessible and of good quality for everyone.

One of the main causes of social inequalities is discrimination. Racial, ethnic, gender, religious or sexual orientation discrimination are some of the many forms of discrimination. These groups are excluded from society as a result of this discrimination, which restricts their chances of fully participating in society. Combating discrimination and promoting equal rights and opportunities for all is essential.

An active intervention is required through public policies, social programs and community actions to combat social inequalities and protect the vulnerable population. By providing vulnerable groups with the ability to overcome obstacles and actively participate in building their communities and lives, these interventions should seek to promote the empowerment of these groups.

Protecting vulnerable people and tackling social inequalities requires the cooperation of various sectors of society, such as governments, civil society organizations, businesses and individuals. These sectors must work together to form new solutions, share resources and promote joint actions in favor of social justice.

Poverty and Inequality

◆ The quest for a fairer world:

Poverty is a condition characterized by the lack of basic resources to meet basic human needs, such as food, housing, education, health and access to essential services. On the other hand, inequality refers to differences in the distribution of income, wealth, opportunities and power in a society. Both are linked to each other and are products of complex social, political and economic structures.

The causes that lead to poverty and inequality are diverse and vary in each nation. Gender discrimination, lack of access to quality education, lack of decent and well-paid jobs, poor distribution of resources, corruption, armed conflicts, unfavorable economic policies for the poorest and environmental degradation are some of the main problems. These elements help to perpetuate cycles of poverty and inequality for generations.

Poverty and inequality are dangerous for societies as a whole and for individual people. Those living in conditions of extreme poverty are the most affected, as they face difficulties in meeting their basic needs, in addition to having limited access to education, health and work opportunities. Inequality also hampers sustainable development, increases crime and causes social tensions.

To fight poverty and inequality, it is necessary to take comprehensive measures and implement integrated methods. Actions that can be taken include:

Invest in high quality education and ensure that everyone has the same educational opportunities.

implement social protection programs such as cash transfers.

promote jobs with fair wages.

guarantees access to health, adequate housing and basic sanitation.

Empowering women and promoting gender equality

Combat tax evasion and implement progressive tax systems.

encourage citizen participation and strengthen civil society.

International Association:

International cooperation is also needed to combat poverty and inequality. Rich countries and international organizations must commit to helping poorer countries with cash, technology transfer and technical support. In addition, it is necessary to ensure that international trade is fair and just, promoting sustainable development and reducing economic disparities between countries.

Marginalized and Excluded Populations

◆ In search of an inclusive society:

Systematic discrimination, social disadvantage and lack of access to basic rights are the result of groups of people being marginalized and excluded. Characteristics such as race, ethnicity, gender, sexual orientation, gender identity, disability, socioeconomic status, national origin or religion can be the cause of this. Opportunities for education, employment, health care, adequate housing and political participation are often denied to these populations, resulting in significant social exclusion.

The reasons why people are marginalized or excluded are complex and interconnected. They include power inequality, prejudice, structural discrimination, entrenched social stereotypes, discriminatory policies, and lack of representation of these populations in decision-making processes. Furthermore, the conditions of these vulnerable groups can be aggravated by elements such as poverty, armed conflict, forced migration and climate change.

Many groups are excluded and marginalized around the world. They include indigenous communities, refugees and IDPs, persons with disabilities, ethnic and racial minorities, women, LGBTQIA+, homeless people, migrant workers, vulnerable children, the elderly and individuals suffering from HIV/AIDS. These communities face various forms of discrimination and social disadvantage, which restrict their access to vital resources and opportunities.

Social and humanitarian implications include:

Marginalization and exclusion have a significant impact on society and the people affected. These consequences include:

A disparity in opportunities: Access to education, employment, health care, adequate housing and political participation are challenges for marginalized populations. This constrains their ability to grow and keeps cycles of exclusion and poverty going.

Aggressiveness and Discrimination: Marginalized communities often experience physical, psychological and structural violence, in addition to experiencing discrimination and stigmatization. This has an impact on their self-esteem, dignity and psychosocial well-being.

Loss of knowledge and diversity: By marginalizing certain groups, we lose the chance to value their cultural diversity, their traditional knowledge and their contribution to social, scientific and artistic development.

Conflicts and social instability: Social exclusion can cause anger, tension and conflict, increasing social instability and undermining peace and cohesion in a community or nation.

Methodologies aimed at promoting inclusion:

Efforts at various levels must combine to promote inclusion and ensure that everyone has the same opportunities. Some useful strategies include: Inclusive public policies: It is essential to adopt policies that promote equal rights and opportunities, protect against discrimination and ensure that marginalized communities are adequately represented in decision-making processes.

Education and Awareness: From infancy, there is a need to fund educational programs that raise awareness of diversity, combat stereotypes, and foster a culture of respect and inclusion.

Economic Empowerment: Ensuring that everyone has equal access to economic opportunities, such as decent jobs, entrepreneurship and microfinance, can help empower marginalized people and help them integrate socially.

Participation and Representativeness: Ensuring that marginalized populations actively and meaningfully participate in decision-making processes at both the local and national levels is essential for their voices to be heard and their needs to be met.

Combating Discrimination: There should be specific laws and policies to combat discrimination such as racism, xenophobia, homophobia and gender discrimination.

Gender and Population Issues

◆ Promoting equality and inclusion:

Gender issues involve inequalities and social constructions that impact people based on gender identity. In addition to biological differences, gender is a social construction that encompasses the roles, expectations and social relationships attributed to men and women. Gender violence, wage disparities, lack of access to education and professional opportunities, and low political and leadership representation are some of the many forms of gender discrimination.

Gender inequality and its consequences:

Society, economics and politics are all impacted by gender inequality. Harmful effects include:

Gender-based violence: Women and people of diverse gender are disproportionately affected by gender-based violence, including sexual assault, domestic violence and human trafficking. This violence has devastating effects on the physical, mental and emotional health of victims.

Economic Disadvantages: Women face wage disparities, limitations in accessing employment and entrepreneurship opportunities, and inequalities in participation in key sectors of the economy. These disadvantages perpetuate female poverty and constrain the potential for economic growth.

Limited access to education: Girls and women still face barriers to accessing education in many parts of the world. Lack of formal education limits their opportunities for employment, autonomy and full participation in society.

Political and leadership under-representation: Women are under-represented in political and decision-making spaces, which compromises the representativeness of their needs and perspectives. This results in policies and laws that do not adequately address demands for gender equality.

Challenges for Marginalized Populations:

Gender issues are extended to marginalized populations such as women in poverty, women of color, women with disabilities, LGBTQIA+ women and people of diverse gender. These groups face multiple and intersectional inequalities, and are more likely to experience discrimination, violence and exclusion.

Promoting gender equality:

A comprehensive and inclusive approach is needed to address gender and population issues. Some methods to promote gender equality include education and awareness. This means promoting inclusive education with a focus on gender equality, breaking down gender stereotypes and learning about the value of respect and equality.

Economic Empowerment: Ensuring that everyone has equal access to business opportunities, jobs, training and credit. This includes policies that increase access to childcare services, equal pay and social benefits.

Political participation and leadership: Encourage women and people of diverse gender to participate in politics and access leadership positions. This requires implementing policies that promote participation and representation, as well as supporting female candidates in electoral processes.

Combating gender-based violence: Create laws and public policies that criminalize and combat gender-based violence, provide support to victims, and try to change harmful customs.

Strengthening human rights: Ensure the legal protection of human rights for all. Respect for sexual and reproductive rights, the end of discrimination and access to adequate medical services are examples of this.

Building a fair, egalitarian and inclusive society depends on gender and population issues. As writers and thinkers, it is our duty to examine these issues and find solutions that foster gender equality, ensure that everyone is included, and recognize each person's diversity and values. The only way to build a society where everyone can live freely, without any discrimination or exclusion, is by working together and implementing inclusive policies.

Conflict, Forced Migration and Refugees

The search for security and dignity:

Civil wars and armed conflicts are a fact in many parts of the world. Millions of people are extremely exposed as a result of these conflicts, which result in large displacements of people. Many people leave their homes in search of safety and survival due to violence, loss of loved ones, destruction of basic infrastructure and lack of access to essential services.

When people or communities are forced from their homes due to conflict, persecution, human rights violations or natural disasters, it is called forced migration. These changes can be internal, when people move within their own countries, or cross-border, when people cross borders to seek asylum in other countries. Lack of adequate shelter, food and water shortages, limited access to medical care and discrimination by host communities are some of the difficulties these forced migrants face.

Individuals who have been forced to leave their home countries due to conflict, persecution or human rights violations are known as refugees. These individuals seek international protection and are protected by international refugee law. However, many people face major obstacles on their journey to safety. They face problems such as discrimination and stigma, as well as lack of access to basic services such as health care, education and work.

Social and humanitarian implications include:

Migration and forced displacement have significant and profound impacts in the social and humanitarian spheres:

Uphold human rights: Protecting the human rights of all people, regardless of their origin or immigration status, is essential. Forced migrants and refugees have the right to safety, dignity and access to basic services.

Solidarity and shared obligation: Countries of origin, transit and destination must work together and collaborate to manage migration flows. To address the complex challenges related to refugees and forced migrants, international cooperation is essential.

Integration and Inclusion: It is essential that host communities encourage refugees to integrate and become part of the community. This includes ensuring access to essential services, creating employment and education opportunities, and fostering cultural respect and mutual understanding.

Trauma and psychosocial assistance: The experiences lived in their countries of origin cause psychological and emotional trauma to many refugees and forced migrants. To facilitate recovery and reintegration, adequate psychosocial care must be provided.

Solutions and Policies: Comprehensive and collaborative approaches are needed to address the challenges associated with conflict, forced migration and refugees:

Conflict prevention: Try to avoid war and the violence that leads to forced displacement by implementing conflict prevention strategies, diplomacy and mediation.

Protection and humanitarian assistance: Strengthen the capacity of humanitarian organizations and international agencies to protect and assist refugees and forced migrants, ensuring respect for their fundamental rights.

Integration and Inclusion: Support policies that help refugees integrate and integrate into host communities, such as access to essential services, employment opportunities, education and training.

Sustainable development: Combat the factors that contribute to conflicts and forced migrations, promoting sustainable development, equal opportunities and the reduction of social and economic inequalities.

Promoting Social Justice and Equality

◆ Building a fairer and more inclusive world:

Inequality can be seen in many forms, such as income distribution, access to basic resources and services, education and employment opportunities, race, ethnicity and sexual orientation. Social justice, marginalization of vulnerable groups and persistence of cycles of poverty are the results of these inequalities.

Inequality affects all aspects of society. It increases social exclusion, impedes economic development and causes social instability. Inequality undermines the fundamental principle that everyone should have the same rights, opportunities and dignity.

Social justice is a principle that aims to ensure that all members of a society receive rights, opportunities and fair treatment. It is based on the recognition of human dignity and the elimination of structural inequalities that prevent certain groups from developing their full potential.

Strategies to Promote Social Justice and Equality: Inclusive Education: Invest in high quality education for all, promoting equal access and incorporating marginalized groups. Education is a powerful tool to promote social mobility, fight prejudice and provide knowledge to individuals.

Redistribution of resources: Reduce socioeconomic inequalities and promote public policies that promote the equitable redistribution of wealth. This can be achieved through investments in infrastructure and basic services, progressive tax systems and income transfer programs.

Empowering Marginalized Groups: Ensuring that marginalized groups participate actively and meaningfully in making decisions that impact their lives. The promotion of diverse leaderships, the guarantee of the rights of minorities and the strengthening of civil society organizations are examples of this.

Eliminating prejudice and discrimination: fighting prejudice, discrimination and stereotypes that sustain inequalities. The promotion of gender equality, respect for cultural diversity, the fight against racism and the guarantee of LGBT+ rights are necessary to achieve this goal.

Strengthening the Rule of Law: Ensure that everyone has access to justice and rights protected. The guarantee of an impartial judicial system, the fight against corruption and the promotion of a culture of respect for human rights are some examples of this.

Issues and commitments:

The promotion of social justice and equality faces several obstacles, including strong economic interests, cultural and political obstacles, as well as low awareness and participation in society. However, to address these obstacles and create an enabling environment for social transformation, governments, international organizations and civil society must commit.

Towards a Sustainable Population Future

◆ Challenges and opportunities:

The world is experiencing rapid population growth. It is estimated that by 2050 the global population will reach 9.7 billion people. The pressure on ecosystems, the scarcity of food and water, the demand for natural resources and the need for infrastructure and basic services for all are some of the challenges that this increase brings with it.

Finding a balance between population growth and the planet's ability to support that population is essential to achieving a sustainable population future. This requires the implementation of policies and practices that encourage the conservation of natural resources, the reduction of excessive consumption, the efficient use of available resources and the shift to clean and renewable energy sources.

To achieve a sustainable population future, the fundamental concept is sustainable development. It includes economic, social and environmental aspects, with the aim of meeting current needs without compromising the ability of future generations to meet their own needs. This includes promoting social equality, defending human rights, protecting the ecosystem and finding new solutions.

Sustainability Chances:

There are opportunities to promote sustainability in a population future, despite the challenges. Some of these chances include:

Education and Empowerment: Invest in high-quality education for all that teaches about sustainability, fosters critical thinking, and empowers people to act in an environmentally responsible manner.

Technology and Innovation: To find sustainable solutions in areas such as renewable energy, low-impact agriculture, waste management and sustainable transport, use technological advances and innovation.

Global Cooperation: Foster international collaboration to address global challenges, share good practices, set common goals, and sign agreements and treaties that promote sustainable action.

Civil Society Participation: Encourage social responsibility and the adoption of environmentally conscious practices, helping the private sector, non-governmental organizations and civil societies to seek sustainable solutions.

Both personal and collective responsibility:

In addition to the opportunities mentioned above, everyone has a role to play in building a future for the population. Public awareness, using public transport, reducing water and energy consumption, recycling and promoting small individual actions can have a significant impact on a global scale.

While this is an ambitious goal, it is possible to achieve a sustainable population future. It requires a global commitment to rethink our consumption patterns, promote social justice, invest in education, innovation and technology, and ensure that all of society participates.

Challenges and Opportunities

◆ Building a future of transformation:

Let's start with the global issues that are shaping our world today. One of them is the climate crisis and the urgency of measures to combat it. Collective and immediate action is needed to address rising greenhouse gas emissions, scarcity of natural resources and dangerous consequences for the environment.

Furthermore, economic and social inequality continues to be a problem in many parts of the world. Human potential is limited by factors such as poverty, lack of access to basic services, social exclusion and disparity in opportunities. These factors also undermine sustainable development.

The rapid technological evolution also brings important problems. On the one hand, AI and automation can change society by improving productivity, efficiency and quality of life. However, these technologies can also cause unemployment, inequality and moral issues.

Furthermore, maintaining privacy and cybersecurity are increasingly important challenges in a digitally connected world. A complex challenge needs to be faced to balance the benefits of technology with the protection of individual rights.

Inclusion and diversity are significant societal challenges that require attention and action. Many societies still suffer from discrimination based on race, gender, sexual orientation and ethnic origin. Addressing these inequalities and promoting equal opportunities for all is necessary to build fairer and more inclusive societies.

Migration and forced displacement around the world constitute another social problem. Millions of people seek refuge in other countries due to increased conflicts, the climate crisis and economic difficulties. Effective migration management and protection of refugee rights are important humanitarian challenges that require a global and collaborative approach.

Opportunities for change:

Despite the aforementioned challenges, it is important to recognize that they also offer us chances to transform a future. Some of these opportunities include: Transition to Renewable Energy: The climate crisis is driving us to look to clean, renewable energy sources such as solar and wind energy. The transition in question will not only reduce greenhouse gas emissions, but will also promote new job opportunities and technological advancement.

Circular Economy: A circular economy, where resources are reused and recycled, increases the chances of sustainable business and reduces waste. Greater efficiency and a more resilient economy can be achieved by promoting environmental sustainability.

Education and Training: To address social and economic challenges, it is necessary to invest in education and training. We can enable everyone to have equal access to high quality education and contribute to a more just and prosperous world.

Technological Innovation: The rapid technological evolution gives us opportunities to innovate in several areas, such as health, transportation, agriculture and communication. The conscious use of technology can help improve people's quality of life, increase efficiency and solve difficult problems.

In an ever-changing world, we face a variety of complicated problems in various facets of life. But it's important to remember that these obstacles also offer us opportunities for change.

Population Policies and Planning Decisions

◆ Building a sustainable future:

In dealing with the challenges and opportunities associated with population growth, governments implement strategies known as population policies. They can cover a range of issues such as fertility, migration, population aging and reproductive health.

A successful population policy depends on accurate demographic data and a good understanding of the population's wants and needs. To develop policies that promote people's well-being, it is essential to consider socioeconomic, cultural and environmental factors.

Planning is a fundamental tool for shaping the growth and development of regions, communities and cities. Access to essential services, the quality of the built environment, transport, infrastructure and other aspects of people's lives can be affected by planning decisions.

Effective and sustainable planning requires an integrated approach that takes into account social, economic and environmental factors. It must take into account equity, public participation and the protection of natural resources to build strong and prosperous communities.

Approaches to Population Policy Decisions and Planning:

Education and Health: Investing in high-quality reproductive health services and education is essential to empower people to make informed decisions about their reproductive lives. Access to prenatal care, contraception and maternal and child health support are important to improving reproductive health and reducing fertility rates.

Sustainable Urban Planning: Developing green areas, promoting efficient public transport, creating accessible public spaces and reducing energy consumption are sustainable urban planning practices that can improve people's quality of life and reduce environmental impact .

Public Participation: It is essential that the community participate in the planning process to ensure that the policies and decisions taken meet people's needs and aspirations. To avoid inequalities and ensure fairness in the decision-making process, active listening, open dialogue and the inclusion of marginalized groups are crucial.

International Cooperation: Population problems are not limited to countries, and global cooperation is essential to deal with common problems. The transfer of information, resources and best practices between nations can result in innovative and sustainable solutions.

Problems and opportunities:

While there are many opportunities to improve the future by implementing population policies and sustainable planning decisions, we also face important challenges.

Resistance to Change: Cultural, political and religious resistance can arise during the implementation of population policies. To gain the necessary support, it is essential to clearly communicate the benefits of population policies and collaborate with community leaders and interest groups.

Limited Resources: Making effective planning decisions often requires sufficient financial resources and institutional capacity. To ensure the effective implementation of planning and policy decisions requires adequate investment in infrastructure, research, capacity building and governance.

Complexity and Interconnections: Policy and planning decisions must take into account the complexity of the population as a complex and interconnected system. Addressing the interconnections between demography, health, education, environment and economic development requires an integrated approach, involving multiple sectors and stakeholders.

Education and Awareness

◆ Transforming lives and building a better future:

One of the most powerful and transformative forces in the world is education. It offers the opportunity to acquire the knowledge, skills and abilities necessary for personal and professional growth. Education also empowers people to become aware and engaged citizens by developing their critical skills, empathy and understanding.

Education is not just in the classroom. It occurs in the family, in the community and in society at large. For social progress, reducing inequality and promoting peace, high-quality, inclusive and equitable education is necessary.

Awareness is the awakening of attention to significant problems that impact human life and the world in which we live. It requires an understanding of human rights, social justice, sustainability, cultural diversity and other issues vital to human survival.

Awareness is a constant process that drives us to think, think and act to improve the world. It allows us to identify and address obstacles, fight discrimination and injustice, and promote positive change in our communities.

Education and awareness put into practice:

Education for All: Promoting equal opportunities requires universal access to high-quality education. An important step to fight poverty, reduce inequality and promote sustainable development is to invest in early childhood, primary and secondary education.

Global Education: Global education addresses global issues and interconnections, transcending national borders. By encouraging intercultural understanding, tolerance and mutual respect, it empowers people to become aware and responsible global citizens.

Environmental Education: The promotion of sustainability and awareness of environmental problems depend on environmental education. It shows us how our actions affect the environment and empowers us to make informed and responsible decisions about how to protect natural resources and the planet.

Media and Digital Literacy: In the information age, digital and media literacy is essential. Active and informed citizen participation depends on empowering people to critically analyze information, understand different perspectives and use digital tools responsibly and ethically.

Problems and opportunities:

Education and awareness have many benefits, but we still have many problems. Obstacles we need to overcome include the spread of false information, educational inequality, lack of access to quality education and resistance to change.

But there are also many opportunities. For example, new forms of access to education and awareness are created by technology, which reduces geographic barriers and expands the reach of knowledge. In addition, unofficial programs such as community programs and non-governmental organizations play an important role in promoting education and awareness in a variety of situations.

A better future depends on education and awareness. They enable people to make smart decisions, fight injustice and contribute to sustainable development.

May education and awareness be recognized and prioritized as powerful instruments to build a hopeful future for human beings.

International Cooperation and Global Goals

◆ Joining forces for a sustainable future:

Pandemics, armed conflicts, poverty and climate change are issues that are not limited to countries. Countries must work together to find effective and lasting solutions to these problems in a collaborative and coordinated way.

International cooperation allows nations to share knowledge, resources and best practices. It promotes economic and social development, strengthens diplomatic relations and promotes peace and stability.

Global goals, such as the Sustainable Development Goals (SDGs), created by the United Nations (UN), offer a comprehensive path for global collaboration. These goals focus on important issues such as ending poverty, ensuring access to education, gender equality, clean energy, social justice and environmental protection.

Global goals serve as a common point of reference that connects nations around common goals. They promote teamwork, sharing experiences and making plans to work together to achieve the intended results.

Benefits of global collaboration:

Knowledge and Technology Sharing: International cooperation allows nations to share scientific, technological and innovation information. This accelerates progress in many areas such as health, agriculture, renewable energy and sustainable development.

Solidarity and Humanitarian Aid: Humanitarian assistance in crisis situations, such as natural disasters and armed conflicts, depends on international cooperation. It saves lives in emergencies and strengthens the bonds of solidarity between nations.

Reducing Inequalities: International cooperation reduces disparities between countries by transferring resources, training and strengthening institutions in developing countries.

Peace and Stability: International cooperation is very important to promote peace and stability around the world. Cooperation between countries facilitates dialogue, negotiation and peaceful conflict resolution.

Challenges and difficulties:

Despite the advantages of international collaboration, we also face major obstacles. Effective cooperation can be hampered by diverging interests, distrust and scarcity of resources.

Furthermore, the strengthening of national nationalism and protectionism can undermine international collaboration. To achieve meaningful results, it is necessary to overcome these obstacles and increase collaboration.

The Contribution of Writers and Intellectuals:

As writers and intellectuals, we play a significant role in advancing collaboration and global goals. We can influence public policy and raise world awareness through our words and ideas.

Dialogue, mutual understanding and the fight against prejudices and stereotypes can be promoted with our influence. We can make voices that are not heard heard and raise urgent issues that need worldwide attention.

Global goals and international cooperation are essential to address the complex and interconnected challenges of the modern world.

Conclusion

This book examines many facets of demography and how it affects the world at large. As a world-famous writer, it gives me pleasure to share my views on this important and complex topic.

Understanding and analyzing population changes around the world depends on demography. Demographic trends help us understand the difficulties and opportunities that arise in various areas and societies.

One of the main conclusions we can draw is that the world's population is undergoing unprecedented change. The current demographic landscape is shaped by migratory movements, aging and accelerated population growth.

These changes bring with them significant challenges, such as the need to provide health and care services for an increasingly elderly population, create economic opportunities for a growing population, and support inclusive policies to address the cultural diversity resulting from migration.

But there are also undeniable opportunities associated with these transformations. The ethnic and cultural diversity caused by migration can benefit societies as it allows for the exchange of different knowledge, experiences and points of view. In addition, population aging can lead to the creation of new economic sectors such as assistive technologies and health care.

Thus, building robust and lasting societies depends on public policies guided by demography. Creating more effective plans to improve the quality of life and well-being of the entire population depends on an understanding of the needs and challenges faced by different age groups, ethnic groups and geographic areas.

It is crucial to highlight that demography is linked to a variety of social, economic and environmental issues. Education, health, housing, work, environment and equality policies are all affected by demographic changes.

Therefore, international cooperation and collaboration are essential to face the challenges and seize the opportunities that arise from global demographic dynamics. Sustainable development and the promotion of global equity can be achieved through the transfer of resources, knowledge and best practices between nations.

It is imperative that academics, politicians and society at large recognize the importance of demography in making choices and decisions in the future. To face the challenges and build a more just, equitable and sustainable future for all, it is necessary to have the ability to anticipate and adapt to the changes that occur in the population.

As a writer, I am privileged to help raise knowledge and awareness of demographic issues. We can help people learn more about demography, talk about it, and work together to create a sustainable population future.

Understanding population changes and creating effective policies to address problems and seize opportunities depend on demographics. We can move towards a more just, inclusive and balanced world by considering the complexity and interconnectedness of demographic issues. Demography is an ever-changing and developing field, so it is our duty as a society to learn, adapt and work together to overcome difficulties and build a better future for all.

Author: Ary S. Jr.

Milton Keynes UK
Ingram Content Group UK Ltd.
UKHW011814041223
433765UK00001B/179